Margaret Benson

The Soul of a Cat

And Other Stories

Elibron Classics
www.elibron.com

Elibron Classics series.

© 2006 Adamant Media Corporation.

ISBN 0-543-86634-3 (paperback)
ISBN 0-543-86633-5 (hardcover)

This Elibron Classics Replica Edition is an unabridged facsimile
of the edition published in 1901 by William Heinemann, London.

Elibron and Elibron Classics are trademarks of
Adamant Media Corporation. All rights reserved.

This book is an accurate reproduction of the original. Any marks, names, colophons, imprints, logos or other symbols or identifiers that appear on or in this book, except for those of Adamant Media Corporation and BookSurge, LLC, are used only for historical reference and accuracy and are not meant to designate origin or imply any sponsorship by or license from any third party.

THE SOUL OF A CAT
AND OTHER STORIES

Photograph by　　　　　　　　　　　Messrs. Kissack

"The Incredible Blue."

THE SOUL OF A CAT
AND OTHER STORIES

BY

MARGARET BENSON

WITH ILLUSTRATIONS BY HENRIETTA
RONNER AND FROM PHOTOGRAPHS

LONDON: WILLIAM HEINEMANN

1901

First Impression, October 1901
Second Impression, December 1901

All rights reserved

DEDICATION TO THOSE DESCRIBED IN THIS BOOK

Once on a time I used to dream
   Strange spirits moved about my way,
And I might catch a vagrant gleam,
   A glint of pixy or of fay;
Their lives were mingled with my own,
   So far they roamed, so near they drew;
And when I from a child had grown,
   I woke—and found my dream was true.

For one is clad in coat of fur,
   And one is decked with feathers gay;
Another, wiser, will prefer
   A sober suit of Quaker grey;
This one's your servant from his birth,
   And that a Princess you must please,
And this one loves to wake your mirth,
   And that one likes to share your ease.

O gracious creatures, tiny souls!
   You seem so near, so far away,
Yet while the cloudland round us rolls
   We love you better every day.

οὐχὶ πάντες εἰσὶν λειτουργικὰ πνεύματα;

PREFACE

> *Prejudice is at first a Guide to Knowledge, but afterwards a Gaoler of Thought.*

THE average Englishman prefers to have his knowledge well formulated and well classified in what one may call a portable and handy form. To such an one it seems desirable to have certain general propositions about the animal creation which, regardless of small subtleties and differences, he may use as a guide for practical action. As, for instance, "that man is governed by reason but the brutes by instinct"; "that the cat, though eminently domestic, is selfish, egotistic, and luxurious; whereas the dog is generous, affectionate, and faithful"; that "cats care for places and not for people."

Many more such maxims may be mentioned,

some of which imply a certain amount of observation, as, for instance, that the parrot possesses an imitative instinct.

Those who have this guide to knowledge will tell you that they like or do not like "the character of the cat," and will ask if you like cats or dogs best.

So some one once asked me whether I liked poetry, and when I asked "whose poetry?" instanced that of the Marquis of Lorne.

But in the first case, too, it would seem to be a relevant point to ask which dog and which cat; and to those who profess not to like "the character" of the cat one might put first the counter-question as to whether they like "the character" of the human being.

As it is well from time to time to compare the best established maxims and formulæ with the results of recent experience and observation; so, although the foregoing principles are extensive enough and fundamental enough to satisfy the greediest grasp after truth, it may not be amiss to compare them with observation of individuals; to compare the general propositions concerning the character of the cat with ob-

PREFACE

servations on certain individual cats ; the common contempt of birds-wits with observation of individual birds ; and to find out the essential point which makes us so certain that similar processes in the man and the brute are in one case the work of reason and in the other case of instinct.

Perhaps we might even come to think that man has some share of instinct, and the brute some dawnings of reason.

Let us face this result boldly, even if it leads us to stammer a little over the irrefragable proposition that, since animals have no souls, this present life contains not only all that they must suffer, but all that they may enjoy ; even if it should make us doubt the perfectness of our scientific grasp of spiritual things, and should seem to lead back to such old doctrines as Peter's belief in the restitution of all things, and St. Paul's hope of the deliverance of the suffering creature into the glorious liberty of children of God.

CONTENTS

The Soul of a Cat	Page 1
Joey and Matilda; or, Intellect and Emotion	17
The Torpid and the Ill-Bred Cat	31
Vanity of Vanities	45
Taffy	55
The Adopted Family	81
The Mysterious Ra	91
Mentu	103
The Conscience of the Barn-Door Fowl	119
Confucius	129
A Paradise of Birds	137
Epilogue	149

ILLUSTRATIONS

Portraits:

    The Incredible Blue   *Frontispiece*

    Persis   *To face p.* 4

    Matilda   ,, 20

    Joey   ,, 26

    The Peacock   ,, 50

    Taffy   ,, 62

    Mentu   ,, 112

    Confucius   ,, 132

IN THE TEXT

Sketches of Cats and Kittens by Madame Ronner

THE SOUL OF A CAT

> *" If you choose to put up with such sufferings as these, I have the power to help you. . . . But bethink you well,"* said the witch, *" if once you obtain a human form you can never be a mermaid again!"*

THE SOUL OF A CAT

Persis was a dainty lady, pure Persian, blue and white, silky haired. When this story opens she was in middle age, the crisis of her life had passed. She had had kittens, she had seen them grow up, and as they grew she had grown to hate them, with a hatred founded on jealousy and love. She was a cat of extreme sensibility, of passionate temper, of a character attractive and lovable from its very intensity. We had been forced to face Persis' difficulty with her and make our choice—should we let her go about with a sullen face to the world, green eyes glooming wretchedly upon it, an intensity of wretchedness, jealousy and hate consuming her little cat's heart, or would we follow Persis' wishes about the kittens, and give them up, when they grew to be a burden on her mind and heart? For while they were young she loved them much. She chose favourites among them, usually the one most like herself, lavished a wealth of care, with anxiety in a small, troubled, motherly face, on their manners, their appearance, their amusements.

I remember one pathetic scene on a rainy evening in late summer, when the kittens of the time were playing about the room, and Persis came in wet and draggled with something in her mouth. We thought it was a dead bird, and though regretting the fact, did not hinder her when she deposited it before her favourite kitten, a shy, grey creature, and retired to the lap of a forbearing friend to make her toilet. But while she was thus engaged we saw that the thing she had brought in was a shivering little bird, a belated fledgling, alive and unhurt. The grey kitten had not touched it, but with paws tucked under him was regarding it with a cold, steady gaze. He was quite unmoved when we took it away and restored it to a profitless liberty, with a few scathing remarks on the cruelty of cats. It is so nice and affectionate of

Photograph by　　　　　　　　　　　　S. A. McDowall

"Persis was a dainty lady."

a father to initiate his little son into the pleasures of sport and show him how to play a fish, but quite another thing for a brutal cat to show her kitten how to play with a live bird—a cat, indeed, from whom we should have expected a sympathetic imagination!

When Persis had washed and combed herself she came down to see how her son was enjoying his first attempt at sport; but no affectionate father sympathising with his boy for losing his fish would have been half as much distressed as Persis to find her kitten robbed of his game. She ran round the room crying as she went, searched for the bird under chairs and tables, sprang on the knees of her friends to seek it, and wailed for the loss of her present to her son.

Again, there was no danger that she would not face in defence of her kittens. My brother had a wire-haired terrier of horrid reputation as a cat-killer. The name or the terrier, for an occult and complicated reason, was Two-Timothy-Three-Ten, but it was generally abbreviated. Tim, large and formidable even to those who had not heard of his exploits, slipped into the room once where a placid domestic scene was in process. Without a moment's pause the cat was on him like a wild beast. I caught Timothy and held him up, but the cat had dug her claws so firmly into his foot that she, too, was lifted off the ground.

But as the kittens grew older maternal tenderness and delights faded, maternal cares ceased, and a dull, jealous misery settled down over Persis. She had been left down in the country with a kitten once—alas! a tabby kitten — which was growing old enough to leave her when I came over for the day and went to see her. The kitten, unconscious of his unfortunate appearance, was as happy as most kittens; he walked round the cat and did not mind an occasional growl or cuff. But she, not responding at all to my caresses, sat staring out before her with such black, immovable despair on her face that I shall not easily forget it.

Thus the cat's life was a series of violent changes of mood. While her kittens were young she was blissful with them, trustful to all human beings; as they grew older she became sullen, suspicious, and filled with jealous gloom. When they were gone she again became affectionate and gentle; she decked herself with faded graces, was busied with secret errands, and intent on æsthetic pleasure—the smell of fresh air, each particular scent of ivy leaves round the trunk of the cedar.

She caught influenza once in an interval of peace and came near dying, and, they said, received attention seriously and gratefully like a sick person; I was not surprised to hear that her friend sacrificed a pet bantam to tempt the returning appetite of the invalid.

While we were homeless for a year or more, Persis was lodged at the old home farm, and lorded it over the animals. Two cats were there: one the revered and hideous Tom, with whose white hair Persis had bestrewn a room in a fit of passion. He had left the house at once for the farm and wisely refused to return. Now he was a prop of the establishment. He killed the rats, he sat serene in the sun, was able to ignore the village dogs and cuff the boisterous collie puppies of the farm. So he met Persis on secure and dignified terms. It was well, for he had formed a tender attachment to her daughter; they drank milk out of a saucer together, looking like the Princess and the Ploughboy; and when the Ploughboy went out hunting (for he must vary his diet a little—unmitigated rat is monotonous) he invariably brought back the hind legs of the rabbit for the Princess.

Strange to say, the Princess was the only one of the grown-up kittens with whom Persis entered into terms of friendship; so while the Princess ate the rabbits of the Ploughboy, Persis ate the sparrows provided by the Princess, and they were all at peace.

She rejoined us again when we settled in a country town. The house was backed by a walled garden; exits and entrances were easier than in the larger houses where Persis had lived with us before. She loved to get up by the wistaria, climb across the conservatory roof, and get in and out through bedroom windows. She found a black grandson already established, it is true, but in a strictly subordinate position. Justice was cast to the—cats, and they fought it out between them; and when Persis threw herself into the fray there could be but one end. Ra liked comfort, but his sensibilities were undeveloped. If he could get the food he desired (and he invariably entered the room with fish or pheasant) he did not care how or where it was given him; a plate of fish-bones in the conservatory would be more grateful than a stalled ox under his grandmother's eye. But to the old cat the attention was everything; she took the food not so much because she cared for it as because it was offered individually to her. If Ra managed to establish himself on the arm of a chair he would remind the owner of his desires by the tap of a black paw, or by gently intercepting a fork. But Persis' sole desire was that she might be desired; the invitation was the great point, not the feast; she lay purring with soft, intelligent eyes, which grew hard and angry if the form of her dusky grandson appeared in the open door. She would get down from the lap on which she was lying, strike at the hand which tried to detain her, and—but by this time Ra had been removed and peace restored.

Her most blissful moments were when she could find her mistress in bed, and curl up beside her, pouring out a volume of soft sound; or when she was shown to company. Then she walked with dainty steps and waving tail as in the old days, with something of the same grace, though not with the old beauty, trampling a visitor's dress with rhythmically moving paws, and the graciously modest air of one who confers an honour. It came near to pathos to see her play the great lady and the petted kitten before the vet. who came to prescribe for her. Now she was all gratitude for attentions, and whereas when she was young she would not come to a call out of doors, but coquetted with us just beyond our reach, now she would come running in from the garden when I called her, loved to be taken up and lie with chin and paws resting on my shoulder, looking down from it like a child. The old nurse carried her on one arm like a baby, and the cat stretched out paws on each side round her waist.

She had more confidence in human dealings, too. I had to punish her once, to her great surprise. She ran a few steps and waited for me with such confidence that it was difficult to follow up the punishment, more especially as Taffy watched exultant, and came up smiling to insist on the fact that he was a good dog.

Taffy's relationship with the cat was anything but cordial. It was her fault, for he had well learnt the household maxim "cats first and pleasure afterwards." But Persis can hardly be said to have treated him like a lady; she did not actually show fight, but vented ill-temper by pushing rudely in front of him with a disagreeable remark as she passed.

All this time Persis was growing old and small. Her coat was thick, but shorter than of old; her tail waved far less wealth of hair. She jumped into the fountain one day by mistake, and as she stood still with clinging hair under the double shock of the water and the laughter one noticed what a little shrunken cat she had become; only her face was young and vivid with conflicting passions.

Then the last change of her life came. We went to a place which was a paradise for cats, but a paradise ringed with death; a rambling Elizabethan house, where mice ran and rattled behind the panels ; a garden with bushes to creep behind and strange country creatures stirring in the grass ; barns which were a preserve for rats and mice ; and finally the three most important elements of happiness, entire freedom, no smuts, and no grandson.

Persis was overwhelmed with pressure of affairs ; one saw her crouching near the farm in early morning ; met her later on the stairs carrying home game, and was greeted only by a quick look as of one intent on business.

The one drawback to this place was that it was surrounded by woods, carefully preserved.

By this time I had come to two clear resolves ; the first, that I would never again develop the sensibilities of an animal beyond certain limits ; for one creates claims that one has no power to satisfy. The feelings of a sensitive animal are beyond our control, and beyond its own also.

And the second was this ; since it is impossible to let an animal when it is old and ill live among human beings as it may when it is healthy ; since it can by no possibility understand why sympathy is denied it and demonstrations of affection checked ; I would myself, as soon as such signs of broken intercourse occurred, give Persis the lethal water. I had been haunted by the pathos in the face of a dog who had been and indeed still was a family pet ; but he was deaf. Even when he was fondled an indescribable depression hung about him ; he had fallen into silence, he knew not how or why. Dogs respond to nothing more quickly than the tones of the human voice, but now no voice came through the stillness. Despairingly he put himself, as they told us, in the way of those who passed, lay on steps or in the doorways. Since we cannot find means to alleviate such sufferings we can at least end them.

But I never needed to put this determination into effect. The last time I saw Persis was once when she came to greet me at the door, and lifting her I noticed how light she was ; and again I saw her coming downstairs on some business of her own, with an air at once furtive and arrogant, quaint in so small a creature.

Then Persis vanished.

She had been absent before for days at a time; had once disappeared for three weeks and returned thin and exhausted. So at first we did not trouble; then we called her in the garden, in the fields and the coverts, wrote to find out if she had returned to some old home, and offered a reward for her finding; but all was fruitless. I do not know now whether she had gone away as some creatures do, to die alone, for the signs of age were on her; or if she had met a speedy death at the hands of a gamekeeper while she was following up some wild romance of the woods.

So vanished secretly from life that strange, troubled little soul of a cat—a troubled soul, for it was not the animal loves and hates which were too much for her—these she had ample spirit and courage to endure, but she knew a jealous love for beings beyond her dim power of comprehension, a passionate desire for praise and admiration from creatures whom she did not understand, and these waked a strange conflict and turmoil in the vivid and limited nature, troubling her relations with her kind, filling her now with black despairs, and painful passions, and now with serene, half understood content.

Who shall say whether a creature like this can ever utterly perish ? How shall we who know so little of their nature profess to know so much of their future ?

JOEY AND MATILDA; OR, INTELLECT AND EMOTION

> "*A thousand little shafts of flame*
> *Were shivered in my narrow frame.*"

> "*But what a tongue, and O what brains*
> *Were in that parrot's head;*
> *It took two men to understand*
> *One half the things she said.*"

JOEY AND MATILDA; OR, INTELLECT AND EMOTION

THE two princesses in the story of Riquet with the Tuft were not more unlike than Joey and Matilda.

The appearance of Matilda is Quakerish, and even shabby. She has an eye like a piece of dull green marble. She is affectionate and polite, but cold and passionless. To judge by the perfect and consistent propriety of her demeanour she might have been a favourite pupil of Mrs. General. Even if she swears or blows her nose she does it with an air of such intense superiority that it seems like an answer in the Catechism.

It is small wonder that Matilda feels superior, for her intellect is supreme. She is not proud of this, for she is too well-bred to wish to dazzle strangers with her brilliance, and her chief flow of conversation is reserved for the circle of her intimates. She came to pay me a visit the other day and was very reticent. "She is too much of a lady to talk to us," my old nurse said; but though she would not hastily confide, she tried to keep up our spirits by a little innocent amusement; and after bleating like a lamb for a quarter of an hour on end, she gave us A flat on the tuning-fork till tea time.

Now, Joey is all green and gold to the eye. He recollects the Valley of the Amazon, and "bright and fierce and fickle is the south." His topaz iris waxes and wanes as the pupil grows large and onyx-like or dwindles to a mere pin's head. He loves passionately, and his hate, deep as the Black Sea, is vindictive and remorseless. Music works in him a frenzy of delight; the sight of friend or foe fills him with an emotion which chokes utterance. Jealousy runs like swift poison in his veins, swiftest and most poisonous when he thinks of Matilda, finished, feminine, and intellectual, a perfect lady.

Photograph by　　　　　　　　　　　　　　S. A. McDowall

"The appearance of Matilda is Quakerish and even shabby."

INTELLECT AND EMOTION

Once, in time long past, there were passages between Joey and Matilda. They were placed side by side, and as Joey looked on that demure Quakeress, her dove colour unrelieved except by two plumes of sober crimson; as he gazed on that marble eye while Matilda huskily and rapidly repeated the name of the kitchen-maid, Joey was aware of an emotion beautiful and strange. Self-control is a foreigner to that hot southern nature, and without a pause for thought he extended a claw—it was all he could do—to the lady.

In a moment Matilda stooped and bit it; and as he screamed with pain and anger she dropped it and burst into a hoarse fit of laughter.

Joey never offended in this way again, but this repulse is the reason of his deep, revengeful jealousy of Matilda.

Another simple scene recurs to my mind. Joey was in the drawing-room, Matilda in a room just above; the doors of both were open. Joey could therefore hear when a passing friend engaged Matilda in conversation. His angry excitement burst all bounds at last, and " Pop goes the Weasel," sung with agonised fervour, came floating up the stairs. Matilda listened with her head on one side, and then sang slowly and impressively a few bars of a species of Gregorian chant. Silence fell below.

Now when they sit side by side they are leagues apart. Joey is viciously watching for any mark of preference given to Matilda, more ready than usual to drive his beak like a sledge-hammer at the finger of the unwary. And Matilda is calmly occupied in observing Joey. Some time in the course of the next seventy years or so she will begin to reproduce Joey; to indicate the way in which he spreads his tail like a fan and grubs in seed and sand, uttering half-audible exhortations to himself, which a stranger would take for imprecations on things in general. How satisfying it would be to an angry man if he could say, "Come on, Joey" in such a tone.

But they do not often sit side by side, for, though you would not think it, Matilda occupies a lower social station than Joey. While his home is in the drawing-room Matilda is the life and soul of the kitchen. Does this humble Matilda? On the contrary; she knows that the true gentlewoman is at home everywhere. If she is brought into the drawing-room she is neither embarrassed nor elate; only a pleasant and discreet reserve takes the place of a free flow of conversation. When she returns to the kitchen she talks rapidly for a long time, and is believed to be describing the things she has seen and commenting on the conversation.*

Alas for the sterner sex! When Joey undergoes an enforced eclipse in the pantry he abandons himself to the situation. He may be heard whistling "Pop goes the Weasel" line by line with his attendant. But this is no honest geniality; for if he is carried back to the drawing-room, and finds waiting for him a friend of higher social station, he turns and bites, if he can, the hand

---

* It must not be imagined that Matilda always confines herself to generalities. She asked a housemaid kindly, "When are you going for your holidays?" And on a rapid entrance and exit of the cook inquired so politely, "And who was that?" that her companion immediately replied, "That was Mrs. ——."

that late has fed him. Perhaps it is Matilda's intellectual interests that preserve her from such vulgarity. She devotes herself to observation for the education of her mind, and when she is not observing she is recording the results of observation. The reproduction of simple sounds comes quickly, for she is a slave to realism. The screams of the peacock, the failing note of the cuckoo, cuck-cuck-oo, the angry mew of the cat, are rapidly and all too accurately reproduced. So, too, the kitchenmaid, before she had served her apprenticeship, was wont to hear her own sad name in corners cried in tones of growing exasperation. We were then living in a town; Matilda's apartment gave on the street, and the errand boys helped her out with the performance.

But, according to the law of her kind, this was a little precipitate of Matilda. She should have let the kitchen-maid grow into a cook; she should have let her live a long and honoured life, and should then have tenderly renewed memories of old days when her name would echo upstairs and down to hurry laggard steps. I cannot decide if this is a want

INTELLECT AND EMOTION

of tact or a supreme instance of tact in Matilda. It cannot, at any rate, be a want of memory, for Matilda has just begun swearing; and as she has been with us for some years, and none of us habitually swear, this must be a sudden revival of memory. It is said to be a very clear and life-like revival.

Probably as for Lovelace, so for Matilda, stone walls would not a prison make, for iron bars do not make any thing like a cage. She drags the door upwards with her beak, and holds it with her claw while she squeezes through like an egg sucked through a bottleneck. This performance drives Joey to the verge of mania. He, too, pulls up his door, but he does not know how to hold it, and it bangs down again and leaves him voiceless with rage, while Matilda is running about as gay as a lark.

But the other day I found Matilda securely imprisoned. Her door was bound with red tape. As mere knots can present no difficulty to an intellect like hers, it was certainly the symbolism which she respected.

Yet with all these qualities of mind and

character, there are one or two points in which Joey excels. Joey wets his sugar. He deliberately dips first one end and then the other into his drinking-trough, and when it is half dissolved he eats it. He tried to soften a piece of wood in the same way the other day — how fruitlessly Matilda knows. Joey has a perch made out of the branch of a tree, and from his perch his toys depend on pieces of string and tape; he owns a cardboard matchbox, and an old tin pencil, and suchlike treasures. One by one he ruthlessly destroys these, so some strings· are always hanging empty. But sitting above them, Joey can test which are empty by their weight, and pulls up only the heavy strings. It is not, however, in practical matters that Joey is seen to the best advantage. His is the artist's temperament; he has a soul for music. Given a braying harmonium and Joey loose, his foes are scattered; but the piano is, so to speak, his forte. "I am convinced," as Lady Catherine de Burgh says, that Joey would have been a delightful performer had his health allowed him to apply. As it is, he attends

Photograph by   S. A. McDowall

"Joey has a perch made out of the branch of a tree."

chiefly to the cultivation of the voice. He seats himself on the shoulder of the meanest performer, or marches up and down from shoulder to wrist; he spreads his tail like a fan; he swells to twice his usual size; his eye goes in and out like the magic-lantern star which sends happy little children to bed with the nightmare. Then the performer plays a weird Scotch air, such as the " Lyke-wake dirge" (one of Joey's favourite pieces), whistling the while, and Joey bursts into song. He does not whistle as when he is performing "Pop goes the Weasel," but he sings with a piercing, strident voice, high and low, pitching with singular skill somewhere near the note, grace notes thrown in according to taste. After Scotch songs give him Wagner hot and loud. In the middle of a performance of the Preislied a stranger once called; but he was happily a reticent man. . . .

But above all there is this: Joey has a heart. It is not a very admirable heart. Its fickleness is beyond description; he hates more hotly than he loves; but the heart is there. He will hear his friend's voice in the house and get mad with anticipation, piping broken fragments of indescribable song. He will follow such an one with low, skimming flight, and will bite any hand except the dearest that tries to bring him back. He is easily deceived—a lovable fault—and a deep voice or a rough sleeve will make him tolerate a woman under the impression that homespun means a man. But where his heart is concerned pretence is vain, and I can imagine Joey dying of a broken heart, though I can imagine him more easily still dying of a bad temper. But Matilda's heart is warranted unbreakable, and is as cold and hard as her marble eye. And I sometimes fear that Matilda is growing a little coarse: a new cook came the other day, and was taken to the cage because the parrot "generally has something to say to a stranger." She burst into a long harangue, of which the only word that could be distinguished was "forget" (it is thought she was declaring her unalterable devotion to the predecessor); but she ended all too plainly, "I don't care for you." Her new hostess firmly replied, "And I don't care for you," upon which Matilda screamed loudly.

INTELLECT AND EMOTION

If there is any truth in re-incarnation, it must be that cynics revisit this world as parrots. The punishment would be horribly appropriate. The man who has disbelieved in the reality of the higher emotions shall have these emotions, but be able to express them only in broad farce. An artist, ardent, vindictive, and cynical has been travestied with the form of Joey. He is animated with the passion which made him plunge his stiletto into an enemy's heart, as in his re-incarnation he tries to drive his beak into a hand. He is met by iron bars and a mocking laugh. Dusk gathers over the sky, that mysterious, familiar beauty stirs his heart; forgetting and forgiving, and he hopes forgiven, he would say good-night to his friends. But the whisper comes in cockney intonation, " Jowey, well, Jowey." He hears the voice of a friend, and would hail him, but " Pop goes the Weasel " rises to his beak. He is kindled as of old by the Pilgrim's March, and bursts into song. But the voice comes hoarse and comic, and laughter greets the kindling eye. All the highest, the best, the strongest feelings of his nature turn in expression into broad comedy, and the reason is that when he was a man he felt these emotions and profaned them by cynicism.

I once met a decrepit old woman who lived on 7*s.* 6*d.* a week. She took a rapid review of the Universe and Life, and closed it by telling me that " things was just about coming to a Grand Pitch." *She* will never be a parrot.

THE TORPID AND THE ILL-BRED CAT

*"Cold eyes, sleek skin, and velvet paws,
You win my indolent applause,
You cannot win my heart."*

They "divided" the time into small alternate allotments of eating and sleeping."

THE TORPID AND THE ILL-BRED CAT

THE torpid cat is really a kitten, but it is of enormous size, and a lively orange in colour. If it lies on the largest footstool it completely covers it, if it occupies an armchair it occupies the whole of it, if it honours the lap of a friend its head must be supported by one arm, while its tail hangs down on the other side, otherwise the centre of gravity could not be preserved and the torpid cat would slide slowly on to the floor and fall like a soft and heavy sofa cushion. It has been lying on a green velvet armchair all afternoon; being temporarily displaced at tea time it fell asleep with its head on the fender; when the chair was relinquished it went back on to it, and it will lie there now till nightfall.

THE TORPID AND THE ILL-BRED CAT

If you catch the torpid cat awake you will find that it has pleasant and intelligent hazel eyes, and a rose-coloured mouth carried half open to be ready for a yawn, as you carry a gun at half-cock waiting for a shot. If you stroke the torpid cat it stretches quietly, but not too far, for fear of waking up.

The ill-bred cat is a small neat English tabby, regularly marked. We made its acquaintance first when it was about six inches long and had come to take charge of the farm. It was sitting on a heap of coals cheerlessly surveying the prospect; when it saw us it sped towards us, crying loud for sympathy and companionship. Then it spied Taffy and went back to the fence to sharpen its claws.

The torpid cat, who was at that time a lively young kitten, and the ill-bred cat made great friends.

In the evening the tabby kitten left the farm to take care of itself, and came up to play with the yellow kitten. They played at being tigers in a jungle. The tabby kitten hid between the asparagus bed and the yew hedge; the yellow kitten sat by the scullery door and pretended that he wasn't looking. Then he began a swaggering walk towards the asparagus bed; the walk quickened as he got nearer, until he was suddenly clawed by the tabby kitten, and the shock of surprise sent him flying into the air like a rocket. Then in the twilight they fled about the garden, crouched in the rough grass beyond the lawn, rushed up the cherry-tree and peered down, all with light, agile movements, until as the light died you could hardly catch the quick rippling of the tabby's stripes, and the yellow coat of the other grew wan.

One morning the tabby came limping and crying from the farm holding out a wounded, swollen paw. She was taken into the house and doctored, but when the paw was well she refused to go home. The two were inconveniently fond of human companionship—the yellow kitten for its own sake, the tabby for a variety of reasons. She grew more emphatically affectionate at meal times.

The yellow kitten used to accompany his mistress to feed the hens; she thought he had an eye for young chickens, but found she slandered him. He was not looking at the chickens;

THE TORPID AND THE ILL-BRED CAT

his ear was open for the rustle of mice in the grass, and from time to time he dashed in and despatched one. He took special pleasure in doing this in company; it was always open to him to hunt in the garden, but he used his privilege when some one was taking the air and inhaling the breath of flowers. He seemed to think it added a point to evening meditation to hear the squeak of the dying shrew or to see an innocent field-mouse untimely cut off while it was peacefully nibbling a blade of grass.

Just so both kittens, with the real self-consciousness of cats, played their games in public; they seemed to have no thought of anything but the mock combat, but the scene of the combat shifted so as to be always under the eye of a spectator. The explanation is simple: the life of a cat is a continuous drama, whether actual or imagined; and what actor will play to an empty house? The cat hunts not for food, but for sport, and the torpid cat, who refused yesterday to look at a mouse let out from the trap, spent the whole of this morning waiting behind the piano with his ear bent to listen to sundry little scratchings.

THE TORPID AND THE ILL-BRED CAT

The cat eats the mouse, it is true; and the sportsman eats venison, but he does not stalk for food.

"Animals," says Mr. Balfour,* " as a rule, trouble themselves little about anything unless they want either to eat it or to run away from it. Interest in and wonder at the works of nature and the doings of man are products of civilisation."

But does this explain why the yellow kitten, as it followed me about the garden, spent some minutes in quarrelling with a pansy? The pansy lifted an inane, purple face towards the sky, and its head waggled helplessly on its stalk. The yellow kitten sat down beside it, and regarded it severely for awhile. Then he slapped its silly face.

A change fell upon the kittens as they grew older. The root of the difficulty was that one had no ancestors at all, and the other only half the proper number. Their voices were too loud, their manners were bad. The yellow cat never mewed, but his purr was like a thrashing-machine; the other was clamorous in pleasure

* " Essays and Addresses."

and complaint, her appetite unquenchable, her demands for affection, for comfort, for food, insistent and unabashed. She would try to drink from the milk-jug while her saucer was being filled; she would run her claws into a hand to get firm hold while she ate the scraps offered her.

If you put her out of the door she reappeared like a conjuring trick through the window; she would jump again and again on the lap of some one who did not want her; she would never take offence. One tithe of the rebuffs she met with would have sent a well-bred cat stalking with dignity from the room; the first of the refusals would have made him turn his back on the company and fall into deep and abstracted meditation. But when her desire was accomplished and the hand weary of hurling her on to the floor, there was something disarming in the bliss on the little impudent face as she nestled in utter confidence and licked the hand that had rebuffed her.

The yellow kitten was less pressing; he had just so much refinement of spirit as to make him refuse to stay in any place where he was forcibly put. He kept his muscles tense, like a coiled spring, and so soon as the grasp slackened quite slowly and deliberately he carried out his first intention.

The two began steadily to deteriorate. Now that the pressure of necessity was removed they were fast losing the stamina of the working cat; and having no sensibilities, natural or cultivated, luxury would never make them aristocratic; they had no education and little discipline, and they gave themselves up to revel in ungraceful comfort greedily and confidently demanded.

Yet their affection for each other, their utter confidence in human nature, lends them a certain grace. You may come into the drawing-room and find the farm cat and the kitchen cat (for such are their real positions) settled in the best armchair. He is lying at luxurious length, sunk in deep slumber. Behind him, squeezed into a corner, sits the tabby; her anxious eyes peer out over his head, her soft little body is crushed by his weight, one tabby paw is round his orange neck. You rouse them and he half awakes; a long paw goes up to draw down the kitten's face to his own; and his rosy tongue comes out and licks her from nose to forehead, then he subsides again into slumber, and her eyes beam out blissful and honoured with the somewhat uncomfortable attention.

Or the little cat has been turned out of the dining-room because of her unceasing demands, and looks in forlornly through the window. Sandy awakes, sees her, gets on the window sill and kisses her through the glass.

Both kittens are entirely fearless with Taffy. Sandy's is a mere absence of fear, greatly due to sleep, and Taffy may wag a tail in his face, just as a friend may flap a handkerchief in it, and yet only induce a flutter of an eyelid. The little cat, on the other hand, is a friend of his, will rub against his paws, and force him to take an ashamed interest in her.

But these are surface tendernesses; the position is fundamentally untenable. A cat must either have beauty and breeding, or it must have a profession.

If it is wellbred it will take a hint; it cannot be disciplined, for a cat is a wild animal, but its very aptness to take offence will bring to it a certain self-control ; if it is a working cat it has its own profession, which occupies it very closely, it has its proper sphere and its own apartments.

There is no help for it. Kindly but firmly the tabby kitten must be induced to return to the farm : kindly, for the mistake is ours. We turned its head, we set it among temptations which its nature could not meet, and we gave it no early discipline. Therefore it must be, like the Cornish nation, led and not driven back. At this age, to coerce is to terrify ; and there is something truly heartrending in looking at the shrinking, furtive air that punishments produce, and thinking of the happy, courageous little beast who sharpened its claws for an attack on Taffy, and gave itself up to the human being in blissful confidence of kind dealing.

Sandy is more of an enigma. One could tell his possibilities better if he would wake up. As he sleeps he grows larger and larger, though few have seen him eat, and he never asks for food. When a teaspoonful of cream is offered him his nose has to be buried in it before he can be roused to drink. He never scratches, he is never angry; when his hazel eyes open he looks with kindness on the company and falls to sleep again. There is only one time in the day when one can be sure of seeing him awake, and that is at prayers. The presence of so many quiet people makes him feel it a good opportunity of amusing them by a little lively play with the bell-rope. If he is put out of the room he seeks an open door or window, and finds a chance of making a fine dramatic rush across the scene, accompanied by the stable cat. Prayers over, his vivacity subsides.

He has a name waiting for him when he wakes, for Sandy is to be glorified into Alexander. But what is the good of naming a cat who cannot hear you through his dreams?

Sometimes I see visions of the future for the two. The first vision is peaceful and prosaic: the tabby is instructing a rustic brood in the art of mouse-catching. She thinks no more of velvet armchairs, of porridge for breakfast and pheasant bones for lunch. Spruce and well-

THE TORPID AND THE ILL-BRED CAT

favoured, the very type of an English cat, guardian of the granary and terror of the mice, she licks her kittens' faces and brings them up to an honest, industrial career.

But there is something nightmare-like in the other vision : Alexander grown to panther size suddenly waking from sleep ; his coat is a tigerish orange, his tail like a magnified fox's brush. What will he do ? Is it torpor only that restrained the heavy paw from striking, and sleep that made the hazel eyes seem kindly ? I find myself looking with a troubled wonder at Alexander as he fills the largest armchair. He is but eight months old—a kitten still.

Postscript.

Alas for Alexander of the pleasant hazel eyes ; for he, too, has fallen a victim to the signors of the night. He was never known to poach, he never brought in a rabbit even, but it is spring, and pheasants are young, and keepers cruel.

So silently Alexander, too, has vanished away, and there is no redress.

VANITY OF VANITIES

" Kind hearts are more than coronets."

VANITY OF VANITIES

I HAVE no clue at all to what the real grievance of the peacock is, though his history, so far as one can piece together fragmentary records, contains all the materials of a tragedy.

Down in the orchard is a great cage made of galvanised wire; a high perch runs across it, and it stands in a sunny, sheltered corner, where it was prepared for the peacock and his hen. Now the galvanised wire is rusty and torn, the woodwork is broken, the cage is patched up now and again to seclude a nesting hen or scratching brood of chickens, or to give temporary lodging to a dainty pair of bantams, and a vegetable marrow ripens its striped gourds in the sunshine. But all alone the peacock, lame on one foot, limps through the farm-yard, and haunts the pigeon tower on the hill; while tradition tells of a day when he alighted on the engine of a moving train, and rumour hints at dark deeds in the past, the scared and blighted life of pea-hen, and a holocaust of young pheasants.

Yet he seems harmless enough, this limping fellow, harmless but embittered. Sometimes evening after evening he will follow me to the fowl-yard and wait for his own portion, drumming out an odd hard note, like the tap of a wooden mallet. Again he disappears, and for days we do not see him. Sometimes he comes to be fed under the windows or at the kitchen door, and will take food even from our hands, but with the distrustful air of one over-persuaded by raisins and lemon-peel.

Sometimes he seems but a mean, faint-hearted creature, running from us with the doubly mincing motion of the lame foot and the horizontal tail, as each separate feather beats upon the air; and again he appears, as when I first saw him, posed for a Japanese picture, high in a flowering cherry with his train, bronze, emerald and indigo, flowing down out of fairy-like clusters of flowers.

But to a peacock " all the world's a stage." If he does but sit meditating at evening on the low garden wall, the flowers below, the dark shrub to the left, the hedgerow elms beyond, with the slope of a field against a primrose sky, all these at once become a fitting background to the crested head and trailing tail. As he stands so, the silhouetted outline shows curves strangely like those of some great cat. Just so Ra's head erects itself; so slope his neck and back, and so the tail lies out in a free curve over the hind leg stretched back. Is there such a thing as a protective outline, and does the silly peacock owe his safety partly to this?

If his very pose is dramatic, much more so is his sudden entrance on the scene. All round the house in summer nights comes the whirring of the owls. Now there seems to be a heavy sleeper under one's very window, now the sound purrs out from the walnut tree across the lawn, now from the bell tower or the ivy on the chimney stack.

So one night we went exploring in the moonlight. Shadows of elms flecked the road where the White Lady is said to ride on November nights. A fir tree stood up in dark masses; thick shadows lay on the grass under the walnut tree. Round the side of the farm buildings an unexpected pool flashed into whiteness; the imagination was on the stretch to see an old owl flap out from under the eaves, and shoot by with silent wing; when suddenly from overhead came a flutter and crash of branches, and a great creature swooped down and fled by with train streaming behind.

It is but seldom he can cause so much sensation; and for the most part he walks alone behind the hedge, peering through at the barn-door fowls, as an anxious exhibitor at a fair peers out from his van to count the sordid crowd collecting.

Towards feeding time, when the fowls begin to gather, the peacock, if he can, pens a few hens into a corner by the woodshed and begins to posture before them, making a harmony of green and gold against the greening lichened wood behind. And the dance, *Il Pavone*, is a

Photograph by   S. A. McDowall

"For the most part he walks alone."

stately affair. He lifts the tail, separating each layer of feathers from the next; each feather of each layer from its neighbour, and the whole train flashes sapphire and emerald. Then with another sibilant shake, feather striking against feather, it is raised upright; the wings showing chocolate wing feathers are drooped almost to the ground, raised and drooped two or three times with a quick flutter, and he begins to turn, conscious that he has an audience behind as well as before. As he turns full face the beauty of outline of the eyeless feathers is made clear; one is apt to think when one finds them, that these are eyed-feathers spoilt; but now they are seen to fringe the entire tail, each ending like a shallow crescent with the horns outwards, so that, instead of the scalloped edging which the eyed patterns would give, these show a fine outline, airy and regular. So raised, too, the fringe up each feather is copper-coloured, the eyes stand out separately in long curved rows, the tail falls away from each side below him in convex curve, and it is here that the feathers with metallic green fringe grow, forming completely a shining curve away from the body. The tail is raised so high that the definite scales of the emerald feathers on the back flow into it; in the front view the wings are hidden. As a single note to a melody, so is the beauty of a peacock's feather to the beauty of a peacock's tail.

Then he turns again towards the fowls, showing to us behind his drooping wings and the skeleton white rays of the feathers on the back. He curves this over his head until it looks like an umbrella turned inside out, and advances upon them with dainty steps; but the fowls dully preen their feathers and run away.

What we call the tail is only the tail covert, and the back view shows the real tail is of stiff feathers, arranged, when these are spread, in an inverted heart shape. Then comes a sudden noise like a loud sneeze, repeated again and again before one can see that it is caused by the sharp striking of the tail feathers against each other and the tail covert—and again he turns and paces.

He made a long solitary parade the other day on the grass, and finally crept through the hedge and into the poultry yard, where we followed him to discover that the whole elaborate proceeding had been carried on for the sake of one dull black hen, in a flurry about the egg she had left behind her.

He was waiting for these fowls the other day while, pending dinner, they had come to dig up a tulip bed. They were routed with ignominy and rushed home past him, indifferent to his presence; and as the pursuer turned he sent out after her an angry, discordant, mocking scream.

The bird is but a false prophet. He screams like a cheap trumpet out of tune when the dog barks, or children shout; and when all is still he fills the air with shrieks, till the superstitious tremble and the scientific say there will be rain to-morrow.

But the morrow rises with cloudless sky and fortunes, and the bird is again discredited. We impute his mistake to the fact that he revels in pessimism.

All of which shows the peacock seen *sub specie humanitatis* and brings us not a whit nearer to what he is thinking, or rather is not thinking, in the small emptiness of his coroneted head. After all, there is very little head, and the tale of a peacock is mainly the story of his tail.

TAFFY

> "The flower of collie aristocracy,
> Yet, from his traits, how absent that reserve,
> That stillness on a base of power, which marks
> In men and mastiffs the selectly sprung."

TAFFY

I

HIS EDUCATION

TAFFY has had an education as many sided as that of a Jesuit. If he was to be sent for at once to Windsor Castle we should not have a qualm about his behaviour, unless, indeed, he should fall, like Guy Heavystone, into " the old reckless mood," in which case he would loaf about the Royal stables when he should be in attendance on the Sovereign.

Taffy entered on the scene as an absurd speckled puppy of three months old. His hair was like tow, and of so strange a hue that when we presented only his back to a stranger he was rarely guessed to be a dog. Some said a rabbit and some a cat; some suggested a lemur, as no one knew what that was like; and some darkly hinted that we were harbouring a young hyæna.

Taffy was brought up in the stables, and early exhibited a lively intelligence. In the gates of the stable-yard there was a little door which opened with a push from the outside. With a spring and a scramble Taffy could get over the gates and would push the little door open for a less agile companion.

With this intelligence Taffy developed an unpleasant temper. "Strange fits of passion" has he known. The first time he saw a bicycle it was being ridden by a harmless little boy. Without hesitation, Taffy knocked down the bicycle and bit the bicyclist.

We all know that intelligence is developed by education, and character controlled by discipline, so Taffy was sent for schooling to a shepherd and coupled with an old, discreet dog. And with regard to this a pleasanter side of his character came to the fore. He had no vulgar pride; for if in later days when he was running with his own horse and carriage he met his monitor, he greeted him with genuine pleasure and respect, and without a touch of patronage. Taffy is a prig, but he is not a snob.

He came home from school, having laid the foundation of his education and learnt to keep his temper. A certain superstructure of cultivation was built upon this, and having (probably) known the pains of the stick, he was now initiated into its pleasures. He learnt to fetch and carry, and retrieve; and such enthusiasm did he show that he began to break branches off trees and uproot tender saplings in the shrubberies.

The next great landmark of Taffy's life was a round of visits. In strict accuracy the round consisted of two visits, and the first visit lasted for eight months; but this acted as a finishing school for Taffy's manners and the turning point of his career. For in this first visit he was taken into the house, and took part in family life. It was a real, independent visit, and Taffy was practically alone, for although Matilda was staying in the same house she was in the kitchen, and could not from the height of her gentility keep a watchful eye on him.

TAFFY

Taffy was so frank and free, so anxious to please and to be pleased, that he was beloved from attic to basement. There was a little boy of his own age for him to play with, and the friends he stayed with knew well how to make a dog feel at home. Indeed, it must be confessed that he still awakes a certain jealousy in the bosoms of his own family by the ear-piercing welcome with which he greets these friends. He still considers their house a preserve of his own; when he went there subsequently with his mistress he gave her a cordial welcome at the front door, and there was something blatant in the way he showed himself at home. He considered it all too literally as a preserve of his own; for, though he was never pressed to join a shooting party, he brought back his bag.

At the next house Taffy rejoined his family, who were proud and pleased to mark the improvement in his manners and deportment. He had fine social qualities, for finding a Dandie Dinmont in jealous possession, he endeavoured to make friends by helping him to the afternoon tea, which had been left on the lawn. Dandie was not tall enough to reach the table, so Taffy handed down a few jam sandwiches on to the grass. This pleasant little incident did not hinder Taffy from knocking down the terrier when he grew quarrelsome, but, having done so, he stood four-square above him, and smiled over the grizzled head snapping helplessly between his feet.

II

HIS COMING-OUT

In the words of the felicitous marriage ode, we may say that for Taffy—

> " Youth's romance was done and over,
> Hail the dawn of serious life!"

But we know that education can never truly be considered as finished, and that when a young lady dismisses her governess she must devote half an hour in the morning to reading Motley's "Dutch Republics," and Mrs. Jamieson's "Italian Painters." Even so when we settled down at last it was unanimously agreed that Taffy must not be allowed to consider his education complete, but must come in every evening to share dessert and enjoy the cultivation of his mind.

As Taffy has "come out," it is time surely to attempt something of a personal description.

Photograph by S. A. McDowall

"Taffy."

TAFFY

He may be described as distinguished in the true sense of the word, for England and Wales have combined to produce a somewhat remarkable blend of colour; luckily they have not quarrelled about the eyes, which are both of the same pleasant brown. His grey, curly back is blotched with black, his legs, cheeks, and eyebrows are a yellow tan. But however opinion may differ about this hyæna-like colouring, all collie lovers would be agreed in admiring his excellent figure, his lithe, agile action, and his well-bred, intelligent head. His family swell with pride as they hear passing remarks on his appearance in the street; they were, in fact, a little disturbed by the glances cast at the rear of their party until they realised that in all the district there was no dog the least like Taffy.

But Taffy is taught to preserve a modest demeanour; he is well snubbed if in excitement over a piece of paper he postures too much, like a dog in a chromo-lithograph—crouching forepaws, a plumy tail wagging, ears raised, and mouth open to show a healthy crimson tongue.

Although Taffy had come out, a strict eye had to be kept on his manners for a time. It was all very well to object to the dustman entering at the garden door. I do not altogether wonder at his entertaining such suspicions of an honest mechanic, who was mending the bells, that he had to be provided with an escort across the garden; it was perhaps even pardonable to give "what for" to a guest who had peevishly declared that he hated dogs. But it was *not* right to bite our landlord, nor to growl at a perfectly amiable visitor at afternoon tea; it was not fair to smell people's boots merely because they were timid, nor proper to close his teeth on the leg of my brother's best friend simply because he had not seen him before. A dog should not growl at housemaids because they want to sweep under the mat he is sitting on, nor should he take offence at being asked to leave the room while furniture is arranged.

But all these things are long past, and it is not well to recall them. Let us only remember that Taffy was always pleasant to ladies, and that if he had to receive a caller he often thought of bringing a pebble from the garden, or a lump of coal from the scuttle to amuse her while she waited. Guests who were staying in the house he would keep happy for hours together by letting them throw sticks for him.

There are a few blacker shadows in Taffy's life, and it will not do to blink them.

It was only the natural, impulsive haste of youth which made him jump through the cucumber frame in pursuit of the sandy cat; but it was a more deliberate indiscretion, a more sinister motive, that moved him to jump in through the garden-room window when he thought no one was indoors.

The old cat had meals served in her own apartment, opening out of the garden-room. This apartment, in which she also slept, was in appearance like a large cupboard, with an easy latch. The garden-room windows were open all the day, and it was not infrequently observed that the cat's plate was polished as by a large wet tongue. Taffy was more than once caught springing lightly into the room ; he assumed a surprised and guilty expression if he found any one there, and hastily withdrew. He was also marked from time to time coming down the passage with the same air of secret satisfaction, mingled with slight apprehension, as on the day when he stole the coachman's beefsteak. So far we could only register suspicious circumstances.

But one evening at lesson time he was missing. We called him all over the house, and heard no strangled whine or scratching paw. At last I went to the cat's cupboard, where a thrilling silence seemed to weigh upon the air. I turned the handle, and, as if shot from a gun, cat and dog burst out together. Oh, the tension of those hours since they had got shut up, and the miracle by which they had both kept their heads! No doubt Taffy, curling through the door with a sinuous, guilty motion, had pulled it after him, and the easy latch had shut, and there they were together, with nerves strained and tense. Taffy, however, to do him justice, had kept cool enough to clean the plate.

Let us turn to a lighter, brighter side.

Taffy, as I said, had no vulgar pride, but he

had to be taught the subtleties of social relations. If he had had a truer instinct on this point he would have saved us from the indignity of seeing him prefer to follow an empty cab with which he was acquainted, to continuing his walk in our company. But he soon learnt discrimination; and though he was very fond of the cab itself, and attached to both horse and driver, he found it better to preserve a certain standard in these matters. Thus with all those whom he did not suspect of base ulterior motives Taffy soon became a mighty favourite. He was known and welcomed on the golf links, at least until his presence became, with his growing ease of manner, a slight embarrassment; he was known in the school, and hailed Sunday with delight, when " Winchester men " came to lunch in order to throw sticks for him and give him catalogues to tear up. He was known in the street, where he would wait outside shops if he were particularly asked to do so; if he was not informed of our intention, he either entered the shop rather rudely or went home. Once he came into the Cathedral, and was so terrified by the vast spaces, the gloom, and the silence, that when his agitated mistress rose from her seat to expel him he fled abruptly to the door and never again entered. For the future he lounged about the Close when we went in, and congratulated us when we emerged from the mysterious, gloomy emptiness.

Once a policeman had to ring his own front-door bell for him; we, cheerfully lunching inside, had not missed him, and did not understand at first why he came in in such a wild bustle of self-importance, crying out, in a high voice, apology and congratulation. He was like a little boy who felt that he had had quite an adventure. It may have been the ready comprehension of this man which gave Taffy so strong an affection for the force. I had to wait at the gaol once when he managed, by repeated blandishments, to scrape acquaintance with the constable on duty. Out of the corner of an eye I watched him laying small offerings of pebbles and sticks at the policeman's feet. As these could not tempt, he sought out a small battered tin toy, which the policeman solemnly picked up and laid aside. Finally Taffy rummaged in the bushes and returned triumphant,

TAFFY

bearing an offering that could not fail to please — a tramp's boot. The man was utterly melted, and with a furtive foot jerked pebbles out of the gravel for the dog to fetch.

The progress of Taffy's lessons was beset with few drawbacks. He learnt the English "Shake-hand" in one lesson, and will give the other paw, or both together, when required. No dog likes to be asked to die for any cause whatever, but Taffy consented to do it, with a sidelong eye and much protest. He jumped with only too much vigour, and was seized with wild desire to lick one's face in passing. He liked to shut the door and sit in a chair, but his energetic performance scratched them both so much that he had to stop. He could hold a piece of ginger-bread in his mouth till he was assured it was paid for, when he swallowed it whole, with a deep sigh and snore. But his supreme performance, requiring an exhausting amount of concentration, is to distinguish between *played for* and *prayed for* and *paved for* and *paid for*. It is at this last only that he eats it, but *paved for* makes him turn his head until he distinguishes the "*v.*" No change of tone affects this; *trust* may be whispered, *paid for* threatened. It requires merely an undivided attention and an unprejudiced mind. If he makes up his mind that *paid for* is coming fourth in the list he stares with stupid eyes at the sound of it; or he eats it gaily at *prayed for* if he is not attending. If people laugh he thinks it funny to eat it at "*parochial*" or "*pantechnicon*." But if he looks at the ground, so as not to catch the eye of light-minded friends; if he turns away his head so as not to be disturbed by the delights of ginger-bread, and if he listens very attentively, he can think.

This is the great value of tricks to the dog, as of mathematics to the man. And Taffy does think; he pauses at an emergency and carries out a plan, simple no doubt, but sufficiently intelligent.

Taffy had a stick too long for convenient throwing, tough and hard. His companion tried to break it, putting her foot upon it and bending it up. When she was tired Taffy pounced upon it, put his paw on it in the same manner, and bent it likewise. Thus they took turns at it till the stick broke. Another long stick was thrown across a gate; he tried to go through the gate holding the stick horizontally, but the bars prevented it; so he took it by one end and dragged it through.

He was accustomed to drop on the ground sticks that were to be thrown for him; but finding that a bicyclist could not reach them, held them of his own accord high up, so that they could be taken from him.

Once in swimming across a stream he was carried down some way by the current before he could land on the opposite bank. He was called back but was afraid to attempt recrossing, and after a pause for thought darted away and crossed a bridge quite out of sight, which his companion had forgotten. Once we had been rolling a ball for him in the conservatory, and it lodged under the plant stands where the tiers were too low to let him through. After trying unsuccessfully to get it he lay down, but when every one else had forgotten the matter, got up quietly and going to a place where the tiers were broken away, walked round under them until he could reach the ball. It is amusing to watch his triumph at having discovered a short cut, hidden from sight, across a loop of road; or his pride in carrying out such a simple stratagem as the following: In the town there lived a gang of five dogs, against whom, of course, no single dog had any chance. We met them while we were driving one day. Taffy saw them first, and, knowing them of old, paused a moment to think. Then he turned and ran, apparently homewards, all five dogs in full cry after him. But it was a gate a little way behind he was making for; he crossed it first and headed off across a field at right angles to the road; he was the fastest runner, and the dogs panted and fell back. When one terrier only remained he turned again, made a long line to catch us up, squeezing through a gap which it would have been madness to attempt with the pack behind him, and rejoined us with cocked tail, looking for applause.

It is this quick intelligence of Taffy's which renders daily intercourse so easy and so pleasant. If he knows you drive daily, the sound of the front door bell at the accustomed time will bring him to the door, to lie gently whining till it is opened. If you have no habit of driving, but tell him the carriage is there, he rushes off to find it ; or you explain to him that it is coming after a time, and he haunts you till the promise is fulfilled. You tell him that he cannot come to church, and he remains behind with downcast, puzzled face ; or you tell him to fetch his hat for a walk (the term has quite reconciled him to his muzzle), and he runs to bring it. It is true that if the muzzle is not in place he may bring any small handy object instead—some one else's hat, the clothes brush, a Bible, or a hand bag, for he seems to regard the action as symbolic. If you feel dull, Taffy will turn out the waste-paper basket and find you a crumpled envelope ; if you are inclined for affection he overwhelms you with demonstration.

In almost every mood or occupation Taffy is delighted to bear you company. There are only two things he cannot stand—one is golf and one is gardening.

III

AN ATTACK OF CYNICISM

Now we took Taffy away from his club life, his beloved cabs, his large circle of friends who threw sticks and catalogues on Sunday, his large circle of enemies with whom he exchanged stimulating defiances in the streets; and we buried him in the country.

He enjoyed the journey, because he knows so well how to behave in the train; he keeps an eye fixed on his mistress, and stays in the carriage or gets out as he is told; he is open to blandishments from respectable strangers, and will lie obligingly on their dresses or rest his head on a knee; he keeps close to one's side on the platform, and gets into a cab as obediently as a child. He liked the new house, too, for the front door was always open, and he needed no kind policeman to ring the bell.

Thus it was a few days before he began to realise the disadvantages. His family was arranging the house, and when he lay genially in the middle of a room he was instantly asked to move. He took offence and went away by himself, but no one had time to call him and rally him on his bad temper. Then he found there were few dogs in the benighted place, and three despicable cats.

But worst of all, an inexplicable change came over the habits of his family; they did not go for drives, and comparatively seldom for walks; but they did foolish things in the garden with rakes, and they fed idiotic hens. They would not even allow him to go into the hen-house to see what was talking so loud inside; worst of all, they played croquet, and his greatest friend putted in the garden.

Taffy loathed the sight of a hoe, of a rake, of a mallet, and of a golf club.

He allowed no ambiguity about the situation; if he saw any one begin to play croquet he turned his back on them and lay down; he refused to go out with a golf club; and if his mistress took the turn towards the poultry yard he went back to the house and lay with a sickened expression outside the front door.

A bored expression began to be characteristic of Taffy. He lay sulkily in front of the house, accompanying for a few steps every one who went out, and turning back as they went straight to some detested occupation.

He got up a fine quarrel with the milkman's dog, but this had only the effect of curtailing his walk, for when two parasols had been fruitlessly broken over the backs of the combatants after morning church, every one felt a little shy of taking him where he might meet the milkman's dog.

The cats were a fresh insult. Two of them were kittens, and not in the least afraid of Taffy, and it seemed to amuse his family to see them rout him; to ask him to look at them, which he could not do for fear of catching their eye; to ask him to kiss them, which he would have scorned to do even if their claws had been less sharp and their tempers more serene.

With these new occupations Taffy's lessons ran risk of being forgotten, so he did not come to the dining-room for dessert. Demonstrations of affection lessened, and Taffy restrained his own outpourings of emotion; in fact he was in danger of becoming a reckless loafer of a dog.

When his family suddenly woke up to the existence of these tendencies in him they tried to mend matters. They paid more attention to his feelings and poured out upon him expressions of affection. Taffy responded with fervour; lessons were begun again, and Taffy presented himself nightly at the dining-room door, singing in a loud, excited tone, greeting the family as if they were a circle of long-lost friends, jerking his head under each arm so as to make it fall round his neck. His best friend took Taffy to sleep in his room, which made Taffy very happy, and he slept nine hours every night and snored most of the time. When the room was unoccupied he slept on the bed and did his best to make it comfortable.

Then a delightful event took the sting from the glorious memory of cabs. Two horses came to the stable, and Taffy could again run down to meet the carriage and place himself underneat', so close to the heels of the horse that he ran considerable risk of having his brains kicked out. There were even advantages in the new arrangement: carriages seemed to go faster than cabs, and there was a stall for him to lounge about. No longer need he repair when he was muddy to a dreary hole, peopled with empty bottles, but to a stall full of crackling straw, to refresh himself by a little horsey society after the insults of the kittens.

And with this change and refreshment of spirits he found himself able to take an interest even in the little tabby cat; he has been seen to lick her face and smell her in a patronising manner. These blandishments generally take place in the garden, and he is embarrassed if they are noticed.

Finally, Taffy resolved to take his part in these restored relations and to try to sympathise with our pursuits. He joined us in a genial frame of mind when we were hoeing a garden path. Every time a weed came up Taffy smelt the place, until his nose was covered with gravel. Finally, when he saw he had grasped the idea of the thing he dug a nice large hole in the middle of the path. So we praised him very much for his kindness and intelligence.

TAFFY

There is no romance about Taffy, and no mystery; we know exactly what he is feeling, and his very secrets are above board. If he has been naughty, guilt is written on his countenance; if he is bored by us, he expresses it as clearly; if has done well, he goes round the circle to collect applause. He lives his life in the full light of day—there are no " silent silver lights and darks undreamed of" about Taffy.

Of course he has his nerves like the rest of us: after a display of affection he seeks a relief from the strain of emotion and repairs quickly to the waste-paper basket; if he is ill it is death to pity him. He becomes unable to raise his head from the ground, unable to swallow; a profound woe is on his face. The wholesome tonic of a few tricks, cheerful conversation, and a little bustle is necessary to restore him. He is now beginning to listen to conversation even when it is not addressed to himself, but he prefers it to have a healthy, objective tone. Talk about good dogs and bad dogs will bring him, self-complacent or apologetic, to your side; but conversation about walks, about carriages and horses he finds far more stimulating. For he is a martyr to self-consciousness; if one tries to draw him he falls helplessly on one side, or moves uneasily, and finally reclines with his head under the sofa. His photographs, too, are apt to wear a deprecating, uneasy expression.

Such is Taffy, intelligent, responsive, lovable, ready to impart his joys and sorrows, thoroughly companionable, entering indeed far more into one's life than is possible for any other kind of animal.

But with all this he is essentially dependent; he is but part of the Red King's dream, and has no thread of existence which is not rooted and twined with human lives; his independent actions are isolated, and the memory of them makes him ashamed and guilty. It is well said that there is no forlorner thing than an ownerless dog; and no unwilling prisoner could love his freedom with such wholeness of spirit as Taffy loves his servitude.

THE ADOPTED FAMILY

*God made all the creatures and gave
them our love and our fear,
To give sign, we and they are his children one family here."*

THE ADOPTED FAMILY

It was quite natural for the peacock to adopt us, for he had been left to his own resources at the farm ; and he preferred bread and cake and poultry food to the pickings of the farmyard. He would come quite close for the bread or the Indian corn, but he would take cake from the hand, thus giving an exact estimate of the value of risk. He paid for these little attentions with his own tail, which he deposited in the course of three days close to the poultry yard.

It was very natural too that the farm kitten should adopt us, her reason being partly real sociable qualities and partly greed and luxury. She liked our company and our cat's company ; she also liked our arm-chairs and our cat's meals.

THE ADOPTED FAMILY

But the adoption by the robins was on altogether a grander scale. They sacrificed family affection and personal safety for the honour and pleasure of domesticating a family of human beings.

We are apt to think of ourselves as occupying this unique position in creation that we alone have the power and inclination to annex other races of creatures for supplies, for service, and for pleasure. If this egotism is at all a matter of congratulation, at any rate we flatter ourselves falsely. The ant keeps its dairy establishment and its staff of domestic servants, or, as we invidiously choose to call them, its slaves. Pumas seem to show a distinct tendency to make pets of human beings, and I strongly suspect that cats take up the same position. We think we have domesticated the cat. What if the cat thinks it has tamed us? It induces us to give it board and longing, and it surely thinks we look up to it with admiration and affection—as we do.

But, above all, robins have a perfect passion for taming mankind.

As far as we know, robins may have tried to

tame other creatures. They may have paid court to cows and horses, but found that they could not catch the eye of a cart-horse, or arrest the attention of the bull. After repeated disappointments (like our own with the zebra) they may have learnt that the only animal really capable of domestication is man.

The decision of the point whether we were taming the robins or they us rests upon this : which side made the first advances.

There was no real question here—the robins began it all.

The robins had been brought up in the ivy of the garden wall. We had played croquet close to them, and gardened beneath them all the summer. They had escaped being raided by the prowling Persian or the orange Angora. Towards the end of the summer the great door into the hall stood open all day, and we used to pull chairs outside into the strip of shade. Then the robins began to take notice of us.

By this time they had grown up and pegged out their own "claims." The baby robin, who had not yet changed his waistcoat, lived in the ivy and sat upon the left gate-post.

THE ADOPTED FAMILY

As we camped opposite in basket chairs he drew nearer, hoop by hoop, across the croquet ground. At last he hopped upon the back of the chair I sat in.

Then we thought it time to return his call, which was most effectively done by the distribution of breadcrumbs.

This caused immediately the descent of the second robin, who lived in a holly tree on the right hand of the door; and at once the feud began. While the baby robin's disinterested attachment had been tolerated, no sooner did he begin to reap a reward than his father swooped on him. We gathered that it was the father, for he was full-fledged, an older bird, neat and smart.

There were altogether four of these robins, and as they adopted the Benson family, what is more natural than to call them by Mrs. Trimmer's beloved names of Robin, Dicksy, Pecksy, and Flapsy. I am convinced that the baby resembled Dicksy; the smart formidable father shall be called Robin; Pecksy and Flapsy have still to emerge.

Now as Dicksy skimmed across the lawn,

THE ADOPTED FAMILY

halted nervously, and advanced to pick up a breadcrumb, like a bolt from the blue Robin fell upon him from the holly tree. Dicksy fled back to shelter, but was received by Pecksy, who, emerging from the arbutus bush, chased him back with a few hard pecks. Pecksy also was half-fledged, and had a queer tuft of light feathers on her head. Although she lived in the arbutus bush, the right-hand gate-post was her watch-tower.

Now since Dicksy had been our first and earliest friend, and could alone be held disinterested, we threw crumbs after him; on these Robin and Pecksy descended; and a crumb happening to fall considerably to the left, out of the left-hand wall came shyly a fourth robin—evidently Flapsy.

The next day witnessed a gourd-like growth of intimacy with Robin. He was always in the near holly tree; he descended for crumbs and came nearer boldly; he even followed us into the house.

But meanwhile Dicksy's life was being made a burden to him. He alone was not allowed to approach us. Pecksy drew nearer, half across the lawn ; Flapsy settled on the croquet stump and took short flights towards us for crumbs ; none interfered with Robin, but Dicksy's appearance was like the trumpet for battle ; each habitat became forthwith an ambush.

Dicksy reconnoitred on the left-hand gate-post—not a robin in sight. He ventured half across the lawn and not a wing stirred. He drew nearer to the tempting crumb, now he was close, and at that moment Robin swooped upon him. Dicksy swerved to the left trying to escape, and Flapsy received him with open beak ; he headed off to the right and Pecksy flew out from her arbutus bush. Finally, he was driven back to cover under ivy leaves with an empty stomach and an unsatisfied heart.

Dicksy must somehow have offended against all codes and conventions of robins, but in what way we grosser mortals cannot conceive.

Later as the winter came on, when Robin came round to the lilac bush at the dining-room window, when he and Flapsy came in to inspect the tables before and after meals, when he entered the bedroom above to inquire after a late riser, and partook of light refreshment, Dicksy still seemed disconsolately to haunt his gate-post.

But now with the coming of spring, and all the new fashions, one cannot be sure of any one's identity. Dicksy, I know, was changing his sombre waistcoat for scarlet ; so I can but hope it may be he who is uttering the quaint little crack of a voice to announce his presence in the next room.

But I tremble for the prospects of next summer if we are going to prove so attractive a family. If Robin and Flapsy nest again in the ivied wall ; if Dicksy brings a mate to the left hand gate-post ; and Pecksy sets up an establishment in the arbutus bush, the war of the worlds will be nothing to the war of the robins.

And at this moment we have undergone a new adoption, for a milk white jackdaw without a tail flew into the garden yesterday, and the household was scattered, uttering endearments, among the cabbages, and scraps of raw meat adorned the lawn. Towards evening he was persuaded to enter the kitchen. Matilda

THE ADOPTED FAMILY

was asked to lend her cage for a time, but when she saw a new centre of attraction she burst into screams so terrific that every one who was not already occupied in housing the jackdaw ran into the kitchen to see who was being murdered. So they provided temporary accommodation for Jack under a basket chair.

He liked it so well that this evening he was found sitting on the chair waiting for some friendly mortal to bestow him inside.

THE MYSTERIOUS RA

*" Reposeful, patient, undemonstrative
Luxurious, enigmatically sage,
Dispassionately cruel."*

THE MYSTERIOUS RA

Rᴀ had three periods of development. In the first, he showed himself cowardly and colourless; in the second, he sowed his wild oats with a mild and sparing paw; and in the third period it was borne in on us that whatever qualities of heart and head he displayed were but superficial manifestations, while the inner being of Ra, the why and wherefore of his actions, must for ever remain shrouded in mystery.

We might have guessed this, had we been wise enough, from his appearance. His very colour was uncertain. His mistress could see that he was blue—a very dark, handsome blue Persian. Those who knew less than she did about cats called him black. One, as rash as she was ignorant, said he was brown; but as there are no brown cats Ra could not have been brown. Finally, a so-called friend named him "The Incredible Blue."

When the Incredible Blue sat at a little distance two large green eyes were all that could be discerned of his features. The blue hair was so extremely dark that it could be hardly distinguished from his black nose and mouth. This gave him an inexpressibly serious appearance.

The solemnity of his aspect was well borne out by the stolidity of his behaviour. There is little to record during his youth except an unrequited attachment to a fox-terrier. In earlier days Ra's grandmother had been devoted to the same dog—a devotion as little desired and as entirely unreciprocated.

But it was necessary that Ra should leave the object of his devotion and come with us to live in a town; and now it became apparent that his affections had been somehow nipped in the bud. Whether it was the loss of the fox-terrier, the new fear of Taffy's boisterous pursuits, or the severity of his grandmother's treatment—for the first time he came into close contact with that formidable lady—whatever the reason may have been, it was plain that Ra's heart was a guarded fortress. He set himself with steady appetite to rid the house of mice, but he neither gave nor wanted affection.

He would accept a momentary caress delicately offered; but if one stroked him an instant too long, sharp, needle-like teeth took a firm hold of the hand. We apologised once to a cat lover for the sharpness of Ra's teeth. "I think the claws are worse," was all he said.

Ra was an arrant coward. If a wild scuffle of feet was heard overhead we were certain that it was the small agile grandmother in pursuit of Ra. If Taffy were seen careering over the lawn, and leaping into the first fork of the mulberry-tree, it was because Ra had not faced him out for a moment, but was peering with dusky face and wide emerald eyes between the leaves.

Once or twice there was an atmosphere of tension in the house, no movement of cat or dog, and it was found that the three were fixed on the staircase unable to move. Taffy looking up from below with gleaming eyes; Granny malevolently scowling from above; and Ra in sight like Bagheera, in heart like a frightened mouse protected by the very fact that he was between the devil and the deep sea. Taffy did not dare to chase Ra for fear of the claws of the cat above; Granny did not care to begin a scrimmage downstairs, which would land them both under the dog's nose. So they sat, free but enthralled, till human hands carried them simultaneously away.

But the general tension of feeling grew too great. Ra's life was a burden through fear, Granny's through jealousy, Taffy's through scolding. Ra was sent off to a little house in London, and here his second stage of development began.

He had always been pompous, now he grew grand. It took ten minutes to get him through the door, so measured were his steps, so ceremonious the waving of his tail. He sat in the drawing-room in the largest arm-chair,

Then it irked him that there was no garden, so he searched the street until he discovered a house with a garden, and he went to stay there for days together. A house opposite was being rebuilt, and Ra surveyed the premises and overlooked the workmen, sliding through empty window-frames and prowling along scaffolding with a weight of disapproval in his expression.

Thus Ra, who had hitherto caused no anxiety to his family, now became a growing responsibility ; visions of cat stealers, of skin-dealers, of cat's-meat men, of policemen and lethal chambers began to flit through the imagination whenever Ra was missing—which was almost always. So to save the nerves and sanity of his friends Ra left London.

We had now removed to the country, and greatly to our regret, though little to that of Ra, his ancient foe had passed from the scene ; and although he felt it better to decline the challenges of the sandy kitten, yet he no longer believed his safety and his life to be in the balance ; it was plain that he had realised his freedom, and would assume for himself a certain position in the household.

The house was a very old one; but Ra had been not long employed before the scurrying of feet over the ceiling was perceptibly lessened, and behind the mouldering wainscot the mouse no longer shrieked. That, indeed, is a lame, conventional way of describing the previous doings of the mice. Rather let us say that the mice no longer danced in the washing basins at night, nor ran races over the beds, nor bit the unsheltered finger of the sleeper, nor left the row of jam-pots clean and empty.

If Ra had confined himself to this small game all would have been well, but he proceeded to clear the garden of rabbits. Day by day he went out and fetched a rabbit, plump and tender, and ate it for his dinner. It must at least be recorded that at this time he was practically self-supporting.

Three he brought to me. The first was dead, and I let him eat it; the second showed the brightness of a patient brown eye, and while I held Ra an instant from his prey, the little thing had cleared the lawn like a duck-and-drake shot from a skilful hand, and disappeared in the hedgerow.

THE MYSTERIOUS RA

The third was dead. I took it and shut up Ra. We "devilled" the rabbit hot and strong; we positively filled it with mustard, and returned it. Ra ate half with the utmost enjoyment and the sandy kitten finished the rest.

Then came Ra's final aspiration. Unwitting of strings of cats' tails, dead stoats, and the gay feathers of the jay, with which the woodland was adorned, he took to the preserves. We have no reason to think he hunted anything but the innocent field mouse or a plump rabbit for us to season; but with a deadly confidence he crossed the fields evening by evening in sight of the keeper's cottage.

If we had all been Ancient Egyptians we should have developed his talent. The keeper would have trained him to retrieve, and he would gaily have accompanied the shooting parties. If I had even been the Marchioness of Carabbas I should have turned the talent to account, and Ra, clad in a neat pair of Wellingtons, would have left my compliments and a pair of rabbits on all the principal houses in the neighbourhood.

Prejudice was too strong for us. I won

truce for Ra until we could find a new home for him, and he departed in safety. I heard, to my relief, that he seemed quite happy and settled, and had bitten and scratched a large number of Eton boys.

Now up to his departure we had at once admired and despised Ra, but no one understood him. His appearance was so dignified, his spirit seemed so mean. He lent a silky head to be caressed, and while you still stroked him, without a sign of warning except the heavy thud of the last joint of his tail, he turned and bit. He addressed one in a small, delicate voice of complaint, yet wanted nothing. He followed me up and down in the garden with a sedate step; there were no foolish games in bushes, pretence of escape, hope of chase and capture. Happy or fearful, sociable or solitary, Ra was utterly self-contained.

Now hear the last act.

Ra began paying calls from his new home, and was established on a footing of intimacy at a neighbouring house. As he sat in the drawing-room window there one morning, he watched the gardener planting bulbs. The gardener planted a hundred crocus bulbs and went home to dinner. No sooner was he gone than Ra descended, went to the bed, and dug up the bulbs from first to last. Then he returned to the drawing-room window.

The gardener came back, and lo! his hundred bulbs lay exposed. Nothing moved; no creature was to be seen but a cat with solemn face and green, disapproving eyes, who glared at him from the window.

The gardener replanted half his bulbs and went to fetch some tool; when he returned he seemed to himself to be toiling in a weird dream, for the bulbs he had replanted lay again exposed and the cat still sat like an image in the window.

Again he toiled at his replanting, and finally left the garden.

In a moment Ra descended upon it; with hasty paws he disinterred the crocuses, and laid the hundred on the earth. Then, shrouded still in impenetrable mystery, Ra returned home.

History does not relate whether or no the gardener consulted a brain specialist the following day.

MENTU

> "*A little lion, dainty, sweet,—
> (For such there be)—
> With sea-grey eyes and softly stepping
> feet.*"

MENTU

Out of the basket there stepped a forlorn little figure, dusky grey, pathetically wailing, cold, hungry, and tired. He was not eight weeks old, every relation and friend in the world was left far behind him; but he was in entire possession of himself and his manners. The ruffled coat was a uniform tint; the little pointed head gave evidence of the long pedigree he trailed behind him. In these weary and destitute circumstances the **true** air of *noblesse oblige* was on him.

His very appetite had deserted him, and for days he had to be forcibly fed with warm milk in a teaspoon. He remonstrated about this, but it impaired not the least his confidence in human nature.

Then he grew **better**, and became an elf-like

creature, playing rather seriously with his own tail, but venturing not far from the skirts of his mistress. Once he saw the old cat, and would have run to her, but she turned on him a look so malevolent that we snatched him out of harm's way, and still scowling she proceeded to take possession of his sleeping basket. She used it for a day or two, but finding that it had been given up to her she abandoned it.

When I joined Mentu and his mistress on a tour in Cornwall some weeks later he had become a different creature. He was still very polite, but had grown in size and in confidence, and he was fast developing the drama of the cat and the madness of the kitten's spirits. He whirled round the room to catch the crackling paper hanging on a string; he played the clown with a cardboard paper-basket, hurling himself into it with such force that it upset and poured him out like water on the other side; he retrieved paper balls, and hanging over the bars of chairs and tables beat them with the tips of his paws; he hid them under corners of carpets and expended an immense amount of time and strategy in finding them again. The paper flew into the air, and sped across the room so fast that only a very clever and agile kitten could ever have caught it. Then Mentu discovered the Shadow Dance.

One evening while the paper was swinging on a string in the lamplight, Mentu suddenly saw the shadow. Thenceforward he renounced the substance and deliberately pursued the shadow. If the actual paper came in his way he hit it with a pettish gesture, and searched the carpet for the shadow. And he knew the two were connected, for at sight of the paper he began to look about for the shadow. Then he rushed after it, and through it; he spread himself out on the carpet to catch it, and it was gone; he fled round and round in a circle after it, and cared for nothing so much as the pursuit of nothingness.

We went to an empty hotel, hidden in a little bay near the Lizard. Green slopes, covered even in March with flowering gorse, fall quickly to the pillared basalt coves. Here you may sit on slabs of rock sheltered from east and north wind, scenting the sweet, pungent incense breath of the gorse, and watching the gulls at play beneath. You can see the great liners pass, signalling at Lloyd's station, and branching off below the Lizard Lights to cross the ocean ; or you can watch the gallant ships come in, corn laden, with men crowding to the side for their first glimpse of English shores. But, except on Sunday, when Lizard Town walks two and two on the cliff, you see no man there and hardly a stray beast.

So here Mentu became the companion of our strolls, scudding across open stretches of green, rushing into shelter from imagined foes under gorse and heather, dancing with sidelong steps and waving tail down little grassy slopes, or lying on ledges of rock as grey as himself, starred with lichen as yellow as his eyes.

Once we went out along the cliff to return by the road, but here Mentu's faith in us deserted him. He set out to go home alone, but dared not ; he wished to come with us, but was tired ; he would not be carried for he saw children in the distance, and a cat prefers to trust its own sense and agility in danger. So in despair of his wavering decision we walked on, until, turning, we caught sight of a pathetic figure silhouetted against the dusty road—a silky kitten with wide mouth opened in a despairing outcry against fate.

Once Mentu met a cow grazing on the cliff. Here was terror, but that he realised the compelling power of the feline eye. He fixed on her two yellow orbs with fear-distended pupils, prepared to make himself very large and terrible by an arched back if she so much as turned towards him, and thus holding her paralysed with terror (though she appeared to graze unconcernedly the while) he walked by with tiptoe dignity and scudded to shelter.

But Mentu himself was once nearly petrified by a very awful kind of Gorgon. He was tripping and smelling, and coming to the edge of a little stone well he looked in. Suddenly we saw him turn rigid, with a face of inexpressible horror. He stood statue-like for a moment, then lifting silent paws retired backwards noiselessly, imperceptibly, step by step from the edge. Once out of sight of the pool he turned and fled. I went to look in. A frog sat there.

Sometimes we went down a stony winding

path to the cove beneath ; a wren was building here, for the cock-wren sat on a bush and girded at Mentu as he passed. One day I heard from far below the sharp note whirring like a tiny watchman's rattle, and returned to find Mentu lying on the path with swishing tail cruelly eyeing the atom which scolded him from above.

When the time came to go home Mentu had undergone another transformation. He had trebled in size ; he had lost the rough, reddish " kitten hair " ; his coat was shining, silky, ashen-grey ; his eyes were the colour of hock. Blue Persians were not plentiful in Cornwall, and a little crowd followed us up and down the platform, for Mentu travelled no longer in a basket.

In the train he was perfectly calm ; looked out of the window at stations, and regarded railway officials with an impartial and critical eye. A fellow traveller pronounced him " a kind of dog-cat," alluding, we supposed, to his intelligent and self-possessed demeanour as he sat upright on his mistress' lap.

We parted again, and from time to time I

had accounts of Mentu. In spring time he relinquished the pursuits of shadows in favour of less innocuous sport. He was found curled up in a blackbird's nest, meditating on the capital dinner he had made of the inhabitants. He laid little offerings of dead, unfledged birds on his mistress' chair or footstool. He was seen trotting across the lawn, his head thrown proudly back, so that the nest he was bringing her should clear the ground. Saddest of all, she hung up a cocoanut for the tits outside her window, and a dead blue-tit was soon laid at her feet.

Again, it was said that he appeared suddenly, like the Cheshire cat, on a tree miles from home; and in early autumn, in the morning, he was seen crossing the lawn with a train of seventeen angry pheasants behind him.

We renewed acquaintance when I came to stay at Mentu's home. He was out when I arrived, and as we sat with open windows in the growing dusk there was a sudden soft leap, and a presence on the window—a wild creature, with shining eyes, the very incarnation of the dusk. Even as he jumped down and came to our feet the mood changed. He purred to us, and went to his dinner plate. Finding there a satisfactory mess he began to eat, turning round to throw rapid, grateful glances towards his mistress, purring the while.

Like the Dean who gave thanks for an excellent dinner, or a moderately good dinner, so Mentu is wont to graduate his grace according to his meat. A fish's head, or the bones of a partridge (it was long before his mistress could be persuaded that he would not prefer a nicely filleted sole) will produce the most grateful glances and the loudest purrs.

As I was occupying the sofa, Mentu took his after-dinner nap on my feet.

It is odd that cats show an intense dislike to anything destined and set apart for them. Mentu has a basket of his own, and a cushion made by a fond mistress, but to put him into it is to make him bound out like an india-rubber ball. He likes to occupy proper chairs and sofas, or even proper hearthrugs. In the same way, the well-bred cat has an inconvenient but æsthetic preference for eating its food in pleasant places, even as we consume chilly tea

Photograph by H. E. Gourlay

"Mentu."

and dusty bread and butter in a summer glade. A plate is distasteful to a cat, a newspaper still worse; they like to eat sticky pieces of meat sitting on a cushioned chair or a nice Persian rug. Yet if these were dedicated to this use they would remove elsewhere. Hence the controversy is interminable.

The next few days Mentu was determined to devote to family life. He came to the drawing-room in the evening and was very affable and polite. He went readily to any one who invited him, and dug his claws encouragingly into their best evening dresses. We had taught him a trick in Cornwall which he still remembered. He lies on his back, two hands are put under him, and he is gently raised. A touch on elbows and knees makes him shoot forelegs and hindlegs outwards and downwards; so that head and forelegs hang down at one end, hindlegs and tail at the other, and the great grey cat lies curved into crescent shape, purring serenely.

In the course of the evening my collie, a visitor with me, came genially into the room. Mentu did not know him; he sat upright, with eyes fixed upon the dog, shaking with terror, but making no attempt to escape.

I heard Mentu calling on his mistress early next morning in a querulous tone. As her door was shut I invited him into my room, but he found it not to his mind, and soon left me. He sat all the morning with us, but was easily *ennuyé,* and walked about uttering short bored cries until he could find some one to play with him. He delighted in a game of hide and seek which he had instituted for himself. He hid and called out, lay still till he was seen, and then sprang up to scud across the room. When we went into the garden he followed, and the scolding of a blackbird made us look up to see him on a branch overhead staring down at us. He walked with us, too, or rather when we walked he plunged rustling through the bushes bordering the path, and flashed out to stand a moment in the open.

Withal one felt that a thinking being moved with us, whether bored or childishly excited, gently affectionate or suddenly grateful.; a being thoroughly self-conscious, greedy of admiration, regarding himself and us, and taking his life into his own hands. And close beneath the surface of his civilisation lay the wild beast nature. One could wake it in an instant, for if I caught his eye the surface flashed sapphire for a moment, then the eye with distended pupils was fixed upon me, and silently, holding me by the eye, he believed, he stole across the room, and jumped up suddenly almost in my face. There was something uncanny about it, and even possibly dangerous, for if I looked up from a book sometimes I found that topaz eye trying to catch and arrest my own, while the great cat stole silently nearer. I think if we had not relinquished the game Mentu's claws would have blinded me.

For the wild nature in Mentu is as strong as his inbred civilisation; and the two are at strife together. His heart and his appetite lead him back and back to the house; keep him there for days together—a dainty fine gentleman, warm-hearted, capricious. But the spirit of the wild creature rises in him, and the night comes when at bed-time no Mentu is waiting at the door to be let in; or in the evening, as he hears the wind rise and stir the branches, even while the rain beats on the window pane, the compelling power of out-of-doors is on him, and he must go; and when the window is lifted and the night air streams in, there is but one leap into the darkness.

He will return early in the morning tired and satiate, or spring in some evening as the dusk gathers, with gleaming eyes where the light of the wild woods flickers and dies down in the comfortable firelight of an English home.

This is the true cat, the real Mentu, this wild creature who must go on his mysterious errands; or who, I rather believe it, plunges out to revel in the intoxication of innumerable scents, unaccounted sounds and the half-revealed forms of wood and field in twilight, in darkness or in dawn. In his soul he is a dramatist, an artist in sensation. He lives with human beings, he loves them, as we live with children and love them, and play their games. But the great world calls us and we must go; and Mentu's business in life is elsewhere. He lives in the half-lights, in secret places, free and alone, this mysterious little-great being whom his mistress calls "My cat."

THE CONSCIENCE OF THE BARN-DOOR FOWL

"The trivial round, the common task."

THE CONSCIENCE OF THE BARN-DOOR FOWL

Few people recognise how strong an element the sense of duty is in the lives of cocks and hens.

I have a Minorca cock of superb appearance and excellent principles. I had to cut his wings once, and I felt as if I had hit a Member of Parliament in the face. It is from him I take my standard.

He receives new hens into his flock with an impressive ceremony. When they are turned into the yard in the approved condition of screaming hysterics, he assembles his old flock about him, and proceeds in a kind of agitated procession towards the newcomers. Then the cock comes a few paces in advance, and with ruffled neck struts and scrapes in front of them. Finally he goes off to the farmyard, the hens following respectfully behind him, the newcomers last of all, pecked and hustled by the rest to make them feel at home.

To his flock of hens the cock stands in much the same position as a hen towards her chickens. It is only the roughness of the instruments they have at hand which misleads us about the particular duty which each is fulfilling.

If a chicken falls on its back it must be remembered that the only instruments by which the hen can help it to regain its feet are a beak and a claw. This is like helping a new-born infant with a sword and a gun. With the full use of ten fingers I feel some anxiety about picking up a chicken. I should quite refuse to do it with a beak and a claw. The hen is braver. She first pecks the chicken to stimulate it to exertion, and then she turns and kicks it. This latter plan is usually the more successful.

But in case of hostilities it must be remembered the hen has only the same two instruments at command. She first pecks her foe and then kicks him. Thus the thoughtless are apt to

THE CONSCIENCE OF THE BARN-DOOR FOWL

confound the different intentions in the similarity of method.

In the same way if a hen, called suddenly from an orgie of herring heads in the farmyard to a meal of corn in her own enclosure, forgets where the gate is and tries to get in through the wiring, the cock has only one possible method of helping her. He flies at her from the other side and pecks her. This is not hostile, but protective ; he is helping her to recover her self-control. When he has succeeded in reminding her that she cannot hope to get through galvanised wire netting he will accompany her politely round to the gate, and bring her to her food.

The range of duties is large. To help thirteen hens to keep their heads in the various emergencies of life is a heavy responsibility ; add to this that the cock keeps time for them, assembles them to their meals, separates fighters, keeps a sick hen away from the flock, or bears a shy one company while she eats ; it will be evident that the self-control of the cock in the matter of food is well matched by his organising ability.

THE CONSCIENCE OF THE BARN-DOOR FOWL

There is only one thing which clashes with the imperative sense of duty of the barn-door fowl, and that is its tendency to romantic attachments.

I had two hens sitting side by side in their first experience of nesting. Daily they were found with dazed faces, ruffled and pecked as we took them out; woke from their angry trance as they felt the earth beneath, took their dust baths, ate, drank, and returned, to fall again into a condition half comatose and half savage.

Thus they spent but twenty minutes daily in the enjoyment of each other's society.

One brood came out five days before the other. The hen was found with an expression of scared surprise on her face, as instead of nine smooth silent eggs, she felt the downy creatures move and heard them cry. She and her brood were removed, and the other sat on with glazed eye till her turn came.

Then we took her also and lodged her next to the first; they had separate dwelling-houses and a common yard. We were only afraid that maternal tenderness would lead to a little pecking of the alien brood.

THE CONSCIENCE OF THE BARN-DOOR FOWL

But it appeared that we had wholly miscalculated. While they sat dreaming side by side or took the refreshing dust bath, those hens had sworn eternal friendship. Although like a Boarding-Out Committee under the Local Government Act, the two hens were individually responsible for both broods, the chickens (unlike the children) were quite a secondary consideration. The hens' main object in life was to sit as close to each other as they could, and the chickens squeezed themselves into corners, roosted on the hens' backs, or moped in isolation.

When one chicken had nearly died of exposure, and three had been flattened under the combined weight of the hens, we removed the worst mother. On this she lost all the little wits she had ever possessed, and haunted the chicken enclosure like an unquiet spirit. It took the cock a long time to restore her self-control.

But I have a far darker tale to tell. There lived in a neat little house on a lawn a gold and red bantam cock with two golden brown hens. The darker was his favourite wife, but the three lived harmoniously, and the hens laid an egg daily.

Fifteen of these eggs were hatched out under a common barn-door fowl. She had no breeding and no tail ; her colour was an undertone of black, irregularly sprinked with grey. She was cooped with the chickens about a hundred yards from the bantams, and screened from them by a shrubbery.

About this time the favourite bantam hen found an attractive heap of faggots : thither she repaired daily to lay an egg. When she had laid a dozen she sat down to hatch them. She had chosen her place well, for her golden brown feathers showed hardly at all against the wrinkled, russet leaves.

While she sat peacefully hidden the cock had heard the hen and chickens call ; and, strolling to the other side of the shrubbery, discovered his fifteen children with their foster-mother. Thenceforward, from morning till night, he squatted near the coop, leaving the little favourite wife in her æsthetic bower, and the paler little wife to her own neat house.

It might be thought that paternal instinct

kept him there, the joy of seeing his young family grow daily more like their mothers and himself; the dawning hope of the time when he should scratch for the young hens and pull the tail feathers out of the little cocks.

Not so; he was enchained by the attractions of that large, common, tailless fowl. Doubtless he thought her a fine large hen; so she was, quite four times his size. Perhaps he admired her figure, and thought her colouring a unique beauty.

Certain it is that just when the little hen was leading out a tiny family, the bantam cock, deserting his two wives and his twenty-seven children, fled with the common hen into the woods.

There they lived in a wild and wicked romance. People passing through the wood at evening might see a very small gold cock and a very large speckled hen sitting side by side on the branch of a tree; or in the morning might catch sight of the pair digging for a precarious livelihood in the grass at the covert edge; glancing round with guilty eyes and fleeing for safety into the bushes.

At last disillusionment came; it was sure to come. The cock went home.

He returned to find *that all the first family were dead and that eight of the second family were cocks.*

This is tragedy, but it is also history.

F. W. COOKE

CONFUCIUS

"Lord! what fools these mortals be."

CONFUCIUS

THE Chow Dog was living in a house on the shores of Loch Lomond ; and the first time I saw him was when he came with his mistress to call at the hotel. For reasons which will presently appear, I shall call him Confucius, though this is not his real name.

When his mistress came in to see us Confucius stopped outside, and I saw him through the window. He was of the shape of a neat little pig ; he was soft and furry, and in colour like a golden fox ; he had black eyes, and a bluish-black tongue. As soon as you saw that tongue you realised how inartistic, how unfinished, a red tongue is ; one might as well have pink boots. By as much as a black Berkshire is more proper and neater than a pink pig, so is a bluish-black tongue better than a red one.

We were so much ravished by the appearance of the Chow Dog that we went out at once to be introduced to him. As soon as he saw us coming he began to trot steadily homewards. We had to leave him to his mistress and retire indoors, and after some conflict of wills and clash of temperaments she appeared victorious with the dog tucked under her arm.

We found that he was at this time only four months old, and absolutely the most self-confident creature living. He thought he knew everything, and scorn was the very breath of his nostrils. Though his personal experience, compared to ours, was short, he felt behind him the centuries of Chinese civilisation. When his empire was elderly, our civilisation was in the cradle. This more than redressed the personal balance and left him to the good.

Confucius clearly did not care to make our acquaintance, but we felt it a privilege to be admitted to a greater intimacy with him.

He comported himself at home with dignity,

Photograph by　　　　　　　　　　　　　　　Messrs. Fall

"Scorn was the very breath of his nostrils."

though not always with civility ; he had none of the puppy *abandon* natural at his age. I tried to teach him to retrieve a piece of paper. He was bored, but he would not be taken at a disadvantage ; so he walked slowly after the paper and gravely returned it to me. After I had persisted in this exercise for some time, he saw that it was meant for a game, and as he would not appear deficient in a sense of humour, he gambolled a little as he went after it.

Confucius never gave himself up to a passing emotion. I saw him once on the rocks with a real puppy, a spaniel puppy bigger than the Chow and probably older. It crouched before him sinuous and silly ; it sprang up, gambolled round him and crouched again ; it flew at a gallop past his nose and lay down on the other side of him. It exhausted itself in futilities, and gasped and panted with its efforts ; and all this time the Chow surveyed it with a bright, contemptuous eye. When it was utterly worn out he got up and went away.

At last Confucius made a mistake. We saw him on the edge of the lake one day with something in his mouth which he swung and tossed from side to side. We called him, and with exultant pride he came towards us. The thing was soft and furry, and so long that it hindered him as he ran. He laid it down before us with jaunty tail and conceited eye—it was his first rabbit.

I had so often smarted under the sense of Confucius' contempt that I was not prepared to be tender to his humiliation. I had not known what it would be like. He took corporal punishment with a fair amount of self-control, but he strained and howled at the indignity of a chain, and the shame of looking at that furry thing of which but just now he had been so proud. When he found that he could not get free, he sat down and thought over the situation until his tail uncurled.

In our walk that evening we were not preceded by a triumphant golden dog, with well-cocked tail and exalted nose, for Confucius followed behind, lost in thought. He did not stray for a moment into the bushes; no rustle of wild creatures could attract him. He was dreeing his weird.

He had finished dreeing it by next morning, however, and his opinion of himself was quite restored—more than restored—as he had laid up a new piece of experience.

The last time I saw the Chow was when we left Loch Lomond. He came with his party to see us off, but it was wet and the boat was late. They had to return home, while we waited sheltering in the pierman's hut.

The party must have fallen out by the way, for we had not waited long before Confucius came trotting back alone, quite cheerful and self-possessed. He went round to the further side of the hut so as to interpose it between himself and the homeward path. Then he sat down very comfortably. If either a dog or a philosopher could have winked, Confucius would have winked at us.

The steamer drew away until the shed grew small against the fir-tree stems, and we could only see a tiny golden speck beside it. But we knew that was Confucius sitting Jacques-like to mock at the world, at our superficial brains, our simple wiles and our infant civilisation.

A PARADISE OF BIRDS

"Oh! the land of the rustling of wings."

A PARADISE OF BIRDS

"' God made the country and man made the town ;' I prefer the latter," wrote a child. Man also made the Suez Canal and the ships upon it, and God made the Salt Lakes and their navies, and most people still agree with the child and prefer the former.

I had heard much about the first, and little about the second, when I landed in Egypt one November and went by train to Ismailia. On the left lay the famous little ditch, and the great ships looking incredibly tiny crept along it ; and on the right lay out the great shallow lakes, and from the edge to the horizon they were as full of feathered fowl as Mother Carey's Peace Pool.

Here in front all over the water were crowds

of little birds, wild ducks maybe, dotted singly, fishing for themselves, and right away lay the flocks of flamingoes, flushing rose as they stood, flashing scarlet as they wheeled, till the flocks on the horizon looked like a sunset cloud. Late in the spring I passed again, and saw not the birds but the reason of the birds. The first time it had been a brilliant, sparkling morning, the second time it was a scarlet sunset. Where the rose-tinted flocks had touched the sky the sun now set behind bars, and where the little birds had floated singly the Arabs were drawing a net—the dark figures, each with his fisher's coat girt round him, stood out against the crimsoned water; as they drew in round after round the silver fish leaped against the meshes, and the sound of their rustling came up to our ears as the train halted.

It is but the lean kine that the Israelites have left in the land of Goshen; yet if I was a tethered beast with scanty pasture I should feel some little comfort in having for company such a vision of whiteness as the paddy bird. To unaccustomed eyes it seems the image of the ibis, though it is not really the same; and it runs in and out over the parched fields, among the heads of the cattle.

There is peace in Cairo now among the Easterns and the Westerns, but there never can be peace between the kites and crows. The feud is carried on in the tops of the palm trees of the gardens. In one fierce contest the bone of contention fell to the ground and I went to find the cause of this eternal feud. It was no more and no less than a dead rat. At the river side they have ample material for contention, and I have seen as many as fifty great hawks or kites together hovering about the masts of the boats.

The kites are seen at their best in a little desert city near. There is not so much noise but that you can hear their musical whistle, and watch their great stately quadrilles in the air, three or four wheeling, poising, passing with swoops and curves against the blue.

A lovelier, more peaceful little bird haunts the palm gardens—the cinnamon and ashen dove which seeks the woods of England in the summer. Ten of them came home by our own boat one spring. They crept on behind it on wearied wing till we pitied them, and hoped they would alight and rest. Suddenly we all saw a sailing ship a mile or two away. With one accord the doves turned and made towards it, but not liking it on nearer view they turned again, caught us up without the least trouble, and again limped along on the wing beside us. But we were comforted for their fatigue.

In November the waters round Cairo had only just gone down, and the fields near Gizeh were all mud. When evening fell there used to come a wedge-shaped flock of pelicans from the desert. The great birds wheeled round the top of Chufu's pyramid, and went off to their fishing.

Each little village up the Nile has its own pigeon tower built four-square, and bristling with sticks for the birds to perch. All the village owns these towers, and round them the pretty flocks clap their wings and take their brisk flights, merry and quick as Arab boys.

The long lines of herons in the water are more typical of the meditative side of Oriental character. They stand out in long grey lines, on long yellow spits of sands in the slow, great curves of the river. But no bird can boast one half the resolute patience of the Griffin Vulture. Round some long curves of the Nile I saw the great grey birds stand; as we drew slowly nearer we could distinguish five, of which two were standing opposite to one another with immense wings spread, ready to fight. When we came opposite it was seen that they were quarrelling about a dead sheep; as we drew away they were still exchanging the *retort courteous, the quip modest, the reply churlish, the reproof valiant and the countercheck quarrelsome;* and we were out of sight again before either gave *the lie direct*. Indeed, for all I know, they may still be typifying the *Concert of Europe*.

The Egyptian vulture is much smaller and much more attractive than this abhorred great bird. *Rachen*, white with black-edged wings, has a beauty of his own as he circles luminously against the sky; there is even a horrid grandeur about him as he springs into sight from the blue, and beats steadily up the wind, allured by carrion scent among the sandhills.

But of all the birds at Luxor the bee-eater is

perhaps the loveliest and the pied kingfisher the most lovable. This kingfisher is dappled white and grey, he poises over water in the position of the dove in stained-glass windows; his wings are lifted fluttering, his head bent down. So he hovers intent and busy, careless of those who pass, till he has perfectly found his aim. Then he drops as a stone falls, the waters close above his head, and in a moment he emerges with a fish curving silver from his bill. If "our loves remain" my spirit will sometimes seek a little horseshoe lake with thick green water, above which sit a parliament of lion-headed goddesses, and there it will watch this kingfisher hover and poise and fall. At this place I once saw our own kingfisher, but he is a travelled fellow and has lost the fearless, busy confidence of the grey native; he does his fishing on the sly, and went by like a blue flash to hide behind some carven stone. And I do not know how soon the pied fisher will learn to follow his example. A German, who thought himself a sportsman, also loved these kingfishers, but, as Browning says, it was "another way of love." He came home one day with a bunch hanging from his hand. I do not know if he took them home and stuffed them to look like nature; more probably he tired of the little grey bodies and threw them away. They would not be so pretty when the soul was gone.

And some men, Englishmen too, have been known to shoot the bee-eater. This is a small light-green bird, as green as growing corn. From its tail hang two long dark feathers; it has a long black beak, with a stripe passing by the eye across paler cheeks. There are some kinds more brilliantly coloured than this; the beauty of it is most manifest when it is bee-eating. Then it spreads bronze wings, turns and flutters like a butterfly, and as it turns a gold sheen ripples over the green. These are sociable birds, and they sit by half-dozens on a branch of carob, taking turns to flutter and catch.

Compared to this bird the crowned hoopoe himself seems almost gross. He is at ease again, since Solomon took back his gift, and the crown of feathers is raised and lowered with a jaunty, self-sufficient air. Where the market road of Luxor ran out into the fields, close by the hole dug by an Arab weaver in the middle of the way to set his loom in, was a favourite place for the hoopoes, and here you might see two or three together, as large as thrushes, with bodies coloured like the russet jay, fine curving bills, and the gay crest. But if you wish to love a hoopoe do not watch it when it eats a thick-bodied moth.

Over the plain of Thebes the swallow plays, glancing by; you hail him as a fellow countryman, but foreign travel would seem to have altered his customs and driven away his dear domestic habits. The old Egyptians carved on stone two little birds like swallows, but one had a wing curled upwards, and one had a straighter wing; and whereas the latter symbolised greatness, the former portended evil. One would need all the wisdom of Egypt to know what mystery lies behind the curling of the wing.

Through the fields another merry bird comes into sight—the crested lark, which is so bold that it will hardly move from the path your donkey takes; or it sits among the corn blades as you go by, and runs but a few steps as you canter past. The birds are tame, because the Arabs do not kill them; Mohammed took a very narrow view of the subject, and it is left to Englishmen and Germans to check the excessive familiarity of birds and men, and to try to make nature more normal.

If these rarer birds are tame, our own bold sparrows are a hundred times more impudent. As the Arab waiters clear away the breakfast they chase the sparrows out through the doors; if you sleep with shutters open you may expect to find a sparrow or two sitting on your bed when you wake; they pry into your cupboard if the doors are left open; they pull a thread out of the mat near your feet to make a nest behind the electric bell wires in the hall; and one determined pair set themselves to build behind the books in our bookcase. We pulled the nest to pieces many times, but they had us at last, and we found two eggs laid upon a wisp of hay.

There is another bedroom visitor with better manners — namely, the little grey owl who mews high up in the palm tree; he does not make himself so common as the sparrow, but in my bedroom one evening he appeared on the window-sill, bowed about a dozen times and went out again.

The wagtails do not come indoors, but outside they will follow and wait for crumbs; will stand with pulsing tail while one lunches at the corner of some temple, running after the scraps of bread thrown to them and waiting to clear the remnants of the feast. The grey wagtail is the commoner, and the plump yellow wagtail is a rare shy visitor. On board ship he catches something more of the spirit of comradeship.

What more can one tell of the cuckoo with spangled crest, whose spangles can be stroked off and come back again; of the chat with rosy breast, of the oriole of golden plumage. The air is still in this country so that you may hear the voices of the past speak silently; and the very song of the birds is hushed in the land of the rustling of wings.

EPILOGUE

*"Imperfect qualities throughout creation,
Suggesting some one creature yet to make."*

EPILOGUE

I

IT is time that the old question of the superiority of cat or dog should be discussed on some other ground than that of British feeling or human egotism.

The case of the cat is prejudged if we are to weigh his merits on practical grounds, for the cat is a dreamer and a dramatist; or if we are to estimate his character from the point of view of Western civilisation, for the cat, as William Watson says, is the type of the Orient; or, finally, if we are to consider the moral qualities of the cat solely in relation to the desires of the human being. If these are our premisses then the vulgar estimate of the cat is the true one.

According to this estimate the cat is a

domestic comfortable creature, usually found curled up like the ammonite, and in a state of semi-torpor; it is essentially selfish and essentially cruel, but apart from these two drawbacks, essentially feminine. "The cat is selfish, and the dog is faithful." This sums up a judgment founded on wilful ignorance and gross egotism.

In respect to what is the dog faithful and the cat selfish? Simply in this regard, that the dog takes the vainest man on something better than his own estimate, while of the cat's life and world the human being forms but a little part.

Here plainly Greek meets Greek, and we had better let the accusation of egotism alone. But apart from this point, the above summary of the cat's nature is about as true as the following summary of the sportsman's nature from the cat's point of view.

"The sportsman is a quiet, domestic creature, fond of his comforts and his meals; he is generally found smoking in an armchair before the fire. The only thing which interferes with his domesticity is his tendency to absent himself from the house for hours together; this appears to be the result of a curious mania quite foreign to his nature; and it will cause him even to miss his meals. If you come upon him at such times he is engaged in a prosaic kind of wholesale slaughter; he has no exciting chases after his prey, no display of ability, no well-planned ambushes; but he kills at a distance through an unpleasantly noisy instrument. The sportsman, too, is absolutely dangerous to life at such time, and I have known cats fall victims to his rage; whereas, if you meet him in his normal condition, he is usually quite tame; you can safely leave kittens in the room with him, and I have never known him kill a caged bird. The keeper is a very dangerous sort of sportsman, and must be regarded as radically unsafe. The difference between sportsmen and keepers is much the same as that between capricious bulls and mad bulls."

The fact is, that the usual judgment of cats rests on a total misapprehension of the scope of a cat's life; and the root of the misunderstanding goes wider and deeper than this. The average human being takes account only of

EPILOGUE

those qualities of animals which have some practical bearing on human life; even the animal lover is wont to take account only of animal qualities, physical, mental, and, at a stretch, moral; whereas that which is the pivot of human life and human relations; that which, rudimentary as it is in animals, is still the pivot of animal qualities—namely, the force of personality—is altogether left out of account.

No judgment of animals can be adequate, or in any sense true, which does not take account of personality, more or less developed, and of the scope of the creature's life as determined by it.

The more intimately one knows animals, the more one is struck by their individuality, and the varying force of their personality.

Persis had the most intense personality of any animal I have ever known. Mentu's, less vivid, was still as individual and distinct; Ra had a little narrow nature, Alexander was undeveloped, and the tabby is frankly common; but all are as distinct from one another, as essentially personal, as five human beings.

And it is greatly through this personality

EPILOGUE

that the scope of an animal's life, as of the life of the human being, is determined; we are all more or less at the mercy of what we, in our blindness, call " blind forces;" but in all of us there is something which out of the " manifold " of the world seeks and selects a consistent experience, some principle which determines the scope of life.

Out of the many chemicals of the soil each plant draws those which are appropriate to its own life, each plant transforms them into a living thing, a definite beauty of leaf and bud.

And the alchemy of the higher creature does not only transform the material particles of the world, now into the ashen silky hair and yellow eyes of Mentu, now into the curly grizzled coat of Taffy; but through the intelligence and sensibilities, through the desire for approbation and of admiration, through the protective love of the offspring, and the pure straining after the affection of the human being, dimly understood, these dawning consciousnesses gather from the world of sensation, of intelligence, of emotion, such material as they can assimilate

EPILOGUE

and transform, defining it into a life and world of their own.

If we cannot from the point of more developed moral consciousness, and higher intelligence, even seek to understand the dawnings in the lower creatures of that which makes us what we are, then to us animals are mere playthings or mere slaves, and we can have no least perception of what is meant by that earnest, if unrealised, "expectation of the creature."

II

*"All instincts immature,
All purposes unsure."*

THE difference between different races of animals appears to lie very greatly in the different scope of their lives.

The cat's life, as distinguished from the dog's, is essentially independent; and this, combined with finer sensibilities and a less facile intelligence, give a predominance in the cat of these elements of character which as developed in the human being we call the artistic temperament.

The cat is, above all things, a dramatist; its life is lived in an endless romance though the drama is played out on quite another stage than our own, and we only enter into it as subordinate characters, as stage managers, or rather stage carpenters.

We realise this with kittens; we see that

EPILOGUE

the greater part of their life, of the sights and sounds of it, are the material of a drama half consciously played; they are determined to make mysteries, and as a child will seize upon the passing light or shadow to help him to transform some well-known object into the semblance of living creature, so you may see the kitten reach a paw again and again to touch a reflection on a polished floor, or conjure the shadows of evening into the forms of enemies.

We cannot but see this, and our mistake comes later when the kitten passes partly out of our ken to reappear from time to time, a serious, furtive creature with the weight of the world on its shoulders. We think then that the romance has ceased, when it has in reality gone deeper; the stage has widened out of sight, and if the cat no longer plays before us it is because we have lost sympathy with this side of its life; if we encourage it, it will play like a kitten up to old age. This same fact possibly explains the reason of the theory that cats care for places and not for people—it may be because these same people care for kittens

EPILOGUE

and not for cats; thus the cat transfers the affection it might have felt for the human being to the scene of its romances and the places where it has experienced the surprise and joy of its kittens.

Corresponding to the dramatic instinct the cat appears to have its sensibilities more developed in the direction of æsthetic enjoyment than the dog's, which are almost purely utilitarian. But it is a strange fact that the most universal kind of æsthetic enjoyment among animals—namely, the pleasures of music—seem to be keenest among those races which comparatively we rank low in respect of intelligence—namely, reptiles and birds.

I whistled "God Save the Queen" once to two green lizards in an Italian garden; they drew by little runs and jerks out of their holes, and their paths converged. Suddenly when their nerves were tense with excitement of the air (rendered slightly out of tune) they saw each other, sprang with one impulse together, bit until I saw the green skin wrinkle, rolled over and disappeared. I have never seen either cat or dog show anything approaching to the

EPILOGUE

emotion which music produces in Joey, though Persis showed some pleasurable excitement in whistling, and some desire to try the notes of a piano for herself. Dogs for the most part take the pleasures of music with extreme seriousness almost amounting to gloom. It is not uncommon to find dogs who will "sing," following to some small extent the air as it rises or falls. But they do this with an aspect of extreme melancholy, and a thrill sometimes seems to run through the whole body before the sound is produced; that they do not absolutely dislike it can only be judged from the fact that they do not try to go away.

Both dogs and cats appear to be unconscious of the sounds they utter until experience has taught them the result or until their attention has been specially directed to it. I have indeed met a Scotch terrier who would "sing" to order, but his face expressed a painful tension of will. To do him justice he sang a strain or two with apparent ease under my window in the middle of the night. Frequently, too, a dog who wishes to make his presence realised has his voice strangulated

EPILOGUE

by nervousness like a shy girl at a music lesson; and a well-bred cat anxious to attract attention sometimes opens its mouth silently.

All such facts seem to point to the conclusion that many animals do not produce their voices voluntarily, but solely on physical impulse; that even imitative utterance may often be based on some such physical sensation, as many people feel a tremble in the throat when a Bourdon stop is on the organ. If this be so we are on the wrong tack in comparing the sounds of animals, however varied and specified they may be, to language, and we should rather compare them to weeping, groaning, sighing, yawning, and laughter, which in the same way produce an imitative response, which are by nature involuntary, and have no tendency to develop into definite language.

If cats and dogs have, compared with other creatures, little feeling for music, they seem to have still less for pleasures of sight. I have known a mare which again and again at the same place seemed to look out with pleasure over a view, when no definite object was moving to catch her eye, but I have never known a dog do this, and though a cat often takes up this attitude, the focus of her eyes seems to be more definitely fixed, and she is probably attracted by some movement too minute to arrest our attention. To colour they seem still more indifferent, not sharing even the susceptibility of the mad bull. I have heard indeed of a dog preferring scarlet to light blue; but it is impossible with a single instance to eliminate individual association. Cats, however, though showing no susceptibility to colour, show a very clear perception of texture. It is not necessarily the most strictly comfortable textures that are preferred; velvet may do to sleep on, but it is on thin crackling paper or stiff silk that a cat would choose to sit, and, above all, to eat. And contrary to all expectation, woolly textures are chosen to lick. A cat has been known to go round the garden in order to lick the soft underside of foxglove leaves; and will even tear a paper wrapper in order to be able to stroke flannelette with his tongue. As flannelette is prepared with a poisonous chemical this pleasure is hazardous.

But the real region of æsthetic pleasure for a

EPILOGUE

cat is the region of smell. The dog uses smell as a medium of information; the cat revels in it. The dog smells the ground to trace friend or foe, food or prey, but the cat will linger near a tree-trunk, smelling each separate aromatic leaf. If the window of a close room is opened the cat goes to it, and puts her head out to sniff the air; she will smell the dress of a friend, partly for recognition no doubt, but apparently partly for pleasure also. An aromatic smell is pleasant; a strong spirituous smell not only disagreeable but absolutely painful. Lavender water or eau-de-cologne may please a tiger but will put a cat to flight.

The cat's drama is a drama of the twilight, when the earth refreshed gives up her secret, subtle scents. It is not to be played in broad daylight; it is a mystery play of things half revealed, subtly transformed, hardly understood, secretly suggestive.

III

" But when she came back the dog was laughing."

COUNTERBALANCING the rudimentary powers of æsthetic pleasure in the cat, we find in the dog a more facile intelligence, and a far more adaptable nature. Some boast that they have taught tricks to a cat; but the fact shows not so much that the cat was intelligent and docile as that its owners were; for their ability has been usually to seize on some natural movement of the cat, in jumping or in sitting up, and gradually to induce the animal to exaggerate it. But the tricks we teach a dog are against his nature, and it needs not only intelligence but docility to take a savoury bite and abstain from swallowing until the precisely right word is pronounced.

A cat walks about with a great purpose dimly imagined in its brain, but a dog plans; he is "the low man adding one to one," but his sums are the most correct, for he is of a practical nature. He does not have to pretend that a stick is alive before he can glean pleasure from playing with it.

How far a dog, or indeed how far any animal is capable of using an instrument for effecting its purposes is an undecided question; but I have heard on near authority of a dog scraping a mat up against a swing door through which he had to pass so that the door was kept open. To use an instrument involves a complicated mental process, in which not only association but reflection on the nature of the thing is required. Taffy associated his muzzle with his walk, and fetched it with pleasure when the association was established; but reflection did not sufficiently come into the process to prevent him from fetching a clothes brush or a Bible instead if convenient.

One clear point of superiority in the dog is his rudimentary sense of humour. Almost any good-tempered dog, when well treated, will try from time to time to laugh off a scolding. If he is encouraged, the fooling is repeated again and again with growing exaggeration as he rolls over with wide mouth and absurd contortions, or flies at one's face to lick it. He appreciates humour in others at his own expense, a thing which not every human being is capable of doing ; if he is teased laughingly, he too will play the fool ; if he is teased cruelly he is cross or wretched. No dog likes one to blow in his face or ear, but Taffy, though not wholly good-tempered, will allow the bellows to be placed even in his mouth if he is assured that it is a game. When the puff of air comes he darts up, jumps at and licks the person who is teasing him, and barks with a wagging tail. If he is really bored or tired he licks the nozzle of the bellows, or the hand that holds them, deprecatingly ; he declines the game, but in perfect good humour.

Now a cat has no sense of humour at all. Its very comedies are serious ; and to tease it is to outrage its dignity. The better bred a cat is the more easily it takes offence. But after all the " sense of the ridiculous " is a gross quality, and the humour of one age or of one class seems vulgarity to another a little in advance. A cat is never vulgar.

IV

*"The tumult of unproved desire, the unaimed,
Uncertain yearnings, aspirations blind."*

IF the scope of life and the qualities of intelligence differ from race to race of animals, the strictly moral qualities appear to differ from individual to individual.

Cats are called "selfish"; but even on the undiscriminating view such qualities differ from cat to cat. Ra was certainly self-absorbed, but I attribute this greatly to unhappy family circumstances when he was young. Persis and Mentu were not selfish in this sense at all. Again and again they have been found in the room with food untouched. When one came in there was a greeting and short display of affection, and not till then would the cat go to its food, and eat with good appetite. Few people think of accusing a straightforward genial collie of selfishness; yet if I left Taffy alone with his dinner, or even with some one else's dinner, there is a strong presumption that I should find the plate clean and shining on return.

What people usually mean by this assertion is that the cat does not, like the dog, depend entirely on human companionship; there are no touching stories of faithfulness to a departed master; there is no overwhelming interest in the human race. A cat has more of what the average Briton calls "self-respect," a quality he likes far better in himself than in others.

On the other hand, a cat has more interest in other races of beings than a dog. The only creatures in which most dogs show spontaneous interest, unsolicited and untaught, are horses; and even here the interest rests on association. But we have all known cases of cats which deliberately set themselves to woo dogs; Ra and his grandmother, unlike in all else, adored the same fox-terrier. I have indeed seen a dog which had lost her puppies nurse a half-grown cat, but the cat seemed to take the initiative. On the other hand, a Manx cat, in a house where I was staying, allowed a beloved terrier to take food out of her mouth. A cat has been known to bring up squirrels; a tomcat of our own fondled and protected chickens; finally, a cat has been known to bring a half-starved friend to share its dinner.

So-called "animal instincts" cannot account for the greater part of these cases, which involve rather definite sacrifice. Dog friendships, on the other hand, rarely involve sacrifice except for the sake of man.

This instinct of benevolence may be noticed among birds. I have heard on good authority of an Uncle canary bringing up a deserted brood, and even with apparent embarrassment taking his place on the nest; of sparrows bringing up young starlings, which, taken from their own nest and placed on a window-ledge, sought refuge in the sparrows' nest; and finally, of a sparrow helping a wagtail to feed a young cuckoo. Unless birds absolutely enjoy filling each other's mouths, such operations involve sacrifice; but in any case there is a large social instinct shown; and when, as I sit in the garden, the bean poles and seed sticks near me begin to blossom into robins, I find I am

EPILOGUE

suddenly the centre towards which such social instincts are directed.

Temper differs in the same way from individual to individual, in extent and quality. Ra had a cross temper; it irritated him if one took liberties, and he struck without warning; but with regard to other animals cowardice kept his temper in check. Mentu had the occasional irritability of a nervous temperament, whether animal or human; he often kept a bold front upon danger, when fear made him afterwards positively sick and unable to eat for some time. Persis was a very fiend to other animals, but had an utterly sweet and grateful temper towards human beings unless jealousy came into play.

Dogs are more often misjudged in respect to temper than cats, probably because their ill-temper is more formidable; and the nervous excitability of the collie is often mistaken for bad temper. I have known a bad-tempered collie, but the clergyman who owned him did not keep him long, as it was apt to make difficulties in the parish if the congregation of the mission church was kept at bay on a dark, windy evening.

EPILOGUE

Pugnacity is perhaps a different thing from ill-temper, and appears to be a very widespread quality in bird-life. A great robin-tamer told me that no robin could support his position unless he was very pugnacious. Those who have tried to tame wild birds, or even those who feed birds in the winter, will notice the extraordinary displays of temper among them; how the blackbird loses half his meal through trying to chase other birds away; how the tits play with him, reckoning on this pugnacity; how the robin after he has made a hearty meal lies in wait for late comers. Barn-door cocks are too universally condemned in respect of temper; my patriarch has been several times reported to me as having placed himself between two young combatants; and he lives on excellent terms with a younger replica of himself, the only point of quarrel being the distance to which the young cock may chase a hen of the other's harem which has strayed into his own yard. Pugnacity is indeed apt to develop into ill-temper with caged birds, but gentle handling in taming and increased freedom would probably go far to obviate this.

EPILOGUE

I have spoken of moral qualities, but the centre of all these is the question of conscience. It is impossible to deny that at any rate the higher animals have conscience, if conscience means the recognition of a law or principle higher than the immediate personal desire and sometimes antagonistic to it.

Even if we allow that the sense of duty in human beings is based on the "sanctions" of pleasures and pain, this makes no difference to the quality of the sense once evolved; neither can it make any difference in the quality of the sense in animals whether this is produced by the "sanction" of nature or of the human race.

The more intelligent domestic creatures accept to some extent a standard given by the power above them. The human standard is to them in a sense as the law written on stone to us; and all know the law has gone forth against the indulgence of ill-temper. Joey recognises this law, and it is a moral effort he makes (very seldom) to refrain from biting; he, too, has a conscience, though a singularly bad one. Taffy with the nozzle of the bellows in his

EPILOGUE

mouth can choose whether to accept the situation cheerfully or crossly.

But the dog accepts his moral code more entirely from the human being than the cat does. In this respect the cat is as the Gentile, without the law, but a law unto himself. There is sacrifice of the lower desires to the higher when the cat brings a friend to share her dinner; when she lets a dog take food out of her mouth; when she carries on towards her kittens, after the immediate needs and desires of motherhood have ceased, a course of conduct more or less consistently educative. A cat, the Egyptians said, reasoned like a man, and this is true in that she determines, like a man, her own ends and purposes in life. It is not approbation but admiration that the cat demands from man; the dog accepts the purposes of life as given from above. But he recognises, as clearly as he recognises the sanction of the gingerbread and the whip, the sanction of moral appreciation or disapproval. He claims applause when he has done well, and when the whip has been endured he still clings with renewed trust to his diviner

EPILOGUE

friend, and seeks by affection to win back approval.

Such animals have wills essentially free as our own, but with dimmer intelligence these wills are more at the mercy of their passions; and the blinder intelligence leaves them, too, more at the mercy of spiritual influences which flow out from us to them. There is a quick response, as with children, not only to our treatment, but to the spirit of our treatment, for they reward our trust with trust, and answer our cheerfulness with heart and courage. And we, too, war with principalities and powers, and are helped in the high and hidden places by influences unseen. We call these creatures blind and unconscious, but our consciousness, too, is dim, and our eyes blinder to things divine than theirs to things human; we both move gropingly and feebly in a great world and battle against the Will that made us and has mercy on us—"so many men that know not their right hand from their left, and also much cattle."

Printed by BALLANTYNE, HANSON & CO.
London & Edinburgh

Printed in Germany
by Amazon Distribution
GmbH, Leipzig